MIRACLES

SCIENCE, THE BIBLE & EXPERIENCE

MICHAEL POOLE

Scripture Union
130 City Road, London EC1V 2NJ

© Michael Poole 1992

First published 1992 by Scripture Union
130 City Road, London EC1V 2NJ

British Library Cataloguing-in-Publication Data
A catalogue record for this book is available from the British
Library

ISBN 0 86201 662 2

Cover design by Phil Thomson

Scripture quotations are from the Holy Bible, New Inter-
national Version. Copyright © 1973, 1978, 1984, Inter-
national Bible Society. Published by Hodder and Stoughton.

Phototypeset by Intype, London SW19 8DR
Printed and bound by Cox & Wyman Ltd, Reading

Contents

Acknowledgments

I am grateful to my colleagues Dr John Martin and Linda Smith at King's College for their helpful comments on an early draft of this book.

My thanks also go to Sue Bond, Celia and Pat Bradley, 'Helen' and her husband, and my wife for reading and commenting on the manuscript.

I should like to record my appreciation of the guidance and editorial work of Sarah Finch and Becky Totterdell.

Michael Poole
Lecturer in Science Education
King's College London

Introduction

Can miracles happen, or is the whole idea of miracles a relic of a pre-scientific age when people were more gullible? Doesn't science show that nature behaves uniformly and, if so, doesn't this rule out the possibility of miracles?

All over the world, and down the ages, there have been claims that miracles have happened. So, are these claims credible? If they are, and miracles *can* happen, do they happen today? If so, why don't they happen more often? And what about the times when they are sought without success?

Broadly speaking, there are two aspects to miracles: the intellectual, which can be debated from the comfort of an armchair or through published papers in learned journals; and the pastoral, which should be approached within the context of church life, with mutual joy or with few words, shared tears and a loving arm around the shoulders.

This book is not a collection of present-day miracle stories, but an enquiry into the miraculous. However, as a starting point, I have used one remarkable event in the life of a friend, in order to explore some of the issues, both intellectual and pastoral.

As we move through the book, different types of chapter

will be encountered; they will cover philosophical, scientific, historical and theological perspectives on miracles. Most of the material is written at a general level, but there is the occasional section where the going is a little tougher.

We shall end with a look at some of the pastoral problems that arise out of dashed hopes and major disappointments.

The conclusion of the study is that miracles are still around today, and that Christians should seek and expect them within the context of the preaching of the gospel, as did the early church. Furthermore, no-one is required to sacrifice their intellectual integrity in order to believe the biblical miracles, including those, like the virgin birth and the bodily resurrection of Jesus Christ, which have attracted considerable publicity in the recent past.

1

Helen's story

I have known Helen Johnson[1] for about twelve years. When I first visited her and her husband, she had her left leg in a calliper, used a wheelchair, walked with crutches and was often to be found slumped on a large cushion on the floor. She had multiple sclerosis.

On the afternoon of Saturday, 10 January 1981, my wife and I were invited to a friend's house to hear a talk about the Christian ministry of healing. The speaker, Tom, believed that God had given him gifts of healing for others, and that it was linked with another spiritual gift known as 'words of knowledge'. Anyone unfamiliar with these and other gifts of the Spirit will find them referred to in Paul's first letter to the Corinthian church, chapter 12, verses 1–11. Tom shared the belief that if God has given someone a 'word of knowledge' he has told them details which they would not otherwise know, the purpose of such a gift being to further, in some way, the kingdom of God.

On this occasion Tom said that one hindrance to our receiving God's healing from illness was the failure to repent of past events and attitudes, and be forgiven. He illustrated the point with real-life examples he had encountered.

Helen's father, an elder from a local church, was there. Helen told me later that he and the other elders had sat up until after midnight the previous night, before concluding that spiritual gifts were not for today; they had ceased with the establishment of the early church.

At the end of the meeting Helen went to talk to the speaker. Meanwhile, the friends who had given us a lift said they had to go, so we left.

A few days later a friend told my wife that Helen had been healed of her MS. We were amazed that such a staggering thing had happened. Apparently, following a private conversation with the speaker shortly after we left, Helen had put down her crutches and, to the horror of her husband, had picked up a tray of bone china and carried it to the kitchen. The expected crash never occurred! But at this stage Helen will tell the story in her own words.

Helen's version

'Following a rather lonely, but moderately happy childhood, interspersed with long bouts of illness, I fell in love with John. We married when I was twenty and after the birth of Sarah, in 1957, I started with inexplicable symptoms of vertigo, pins and needles and a generally exhausted feeling. These almost passed and by the age of twenty-two I was delighted to find that baby number two was on the way. During Tracy's birth these unexplained symptoms came back, again accompanied by constant tiredness and weakness. I began to despair of ever feeling well again, when I realised that our third child was soon to be expected. During this time my husband, a city banker, was approached to become a lay pastor in a village church near Southampton. Shortly after Barry's birth our family moved and I again became part of a church leader's family – my father having been an elder in the Brethren Church, and now my husband a pastor in a free church.

Following Barry's birth I became depressed and extremely anxious. I attempted suicide twice, partly due to always feeling physically ill. Eventually after hospitalisation and many more months of illness my local doctor diagnosed multiple sclerosis and I entered the National Hospital for Nervous Diseases in London. During this time of great spiritual questioning I went for counselling and, amidst the pain and discomfort of disability, I had a vision of the Lord Jesus Christ with outstretched arms telling me that he loved me. I was given the gift of tongues [see 1 Corinthians 12 again] and filled with great peace and joy.

In January 1981 John and I approached the London Healing Mission and asked the chaplain to come and speak on healing to a church-based group.

After the main meeting had concluded Tom wanted to know if I would like him to pray for me. I was hesitant, because of my shyness, but I felt honoured that he should want to pray. Tom assured me that he would pray for my healing, but first he had to tell me that the Lord had given him a word of knowledge concerning my condition. I knew, at this moment of time, that the Lord had surely spoken to Tom about me and when I was asked if I had always wanted attention I had to be honest and agree. After a brief prayer of confession and asking for forgiveness, Tom then asked the Lord to take away the spirit of infirmity of multiple sclerosis. Immediately I knew that the Lord had healed me, though I had felt nothing, and the realisation of being well began to dawn on me.

As Tom was leaving to catch a train, I looked down at my elbow crutches and suddenly asked, "If I am healed – I won't need to use my crutches and wheelchair again, will I?" Tom's answer was that if I believed God had healed me, why should I need to use the crutches? Tom left the living room and I was alone to pray and ask God for guidance for the next step. I felt him tell me to stand up, unaided, and walk to the opposite side of the room, pick up a tray of bone china mugs and carry them out to the kitchen. This I did, and being faithless, was amazed at how easy this action was. My healing had started that day and was to go on during the next week until my husband bought me a cycle so that, at last, we could go out together. All the glory is due to God.

It was very difficult to persuade the doctors to accept back my mobility allowance but easy to find a buyer for the two wheelchairs. Within two weeks I was riding a new bicycle and swimming lengths of the pool.

Some ten years have now passed and I have never felt any MS symptoms return and can still praise God for his healing power today. It amazes me that the Lord can take a disabled housewife and, through healing her, turn her into a minister's wife, running a wholefood coffee shop in the local church. When my husband became a full-time Baptist minister in 1985 we both wanted to be used by the Lord in any way for his service, and we are often asked to pray for people's healing and problems. Physically I go fitness training weekly and running most mornings, and continue to praise him during the hard times and the times of blessings.'

The sequel

When, in New Testament times, the news got around that a crippled man had been healed (see the story in Acts 3), the man's neighbours were 'filled with wonder and amazement at what had happened'. It was similar in Helen's case: 'Hey! isn't that Helen cycling past? It *can't* be!' Everyone found it difficult to believe, for a while, especially Helen herself and her family. It seemed so unreal. But after seeing Helen a few times one just had to take on board what one's senses were shouting so loudly. The event seemed to be tied up with something 'spiritual', for want of a better word. So it did not seem to be a case of 'spontaneous remission' – a medical term for 'better, but we haven't a clue why'.

I have in front of me a photocopy of a letter Helen wrote on 3 April 1981 to the Department of Health and Social Security. It reads:

Dear Sir,
I am notifying your department that I am now able to walk unaided for at least 3 miles and do not consider myself to be suffering from Multiple Sclerosis any more. I have reported to my physician who has reserved judgment. Will you inform me if I should return my book [Mobility Allowance Pension Book] to you.
            Yours faithfully,
            Helen Johnson

A cautious medical report written on 11 August 1981 by Helen's GP states:

Several months ago this patient attended my Surgery to report that she had been totally cured of her condition, and at that time I could see no residual evidence of disability.

    With regard to prognosis I am optimistic that the present situation will be maintained . . .

Of course I asked Helen how her healing had affected her father's belief that spiritual gifts were not for today. Did God have a sense of humour, I wondered, healing his daughter the day after the elders had deliberated so long into the night before concluding that such gifts finished with the apostles?

Naively I thought that no one could maintain such a position in the face of so clear a rebuttal. Now, I think I should have anticipated that he would do so. If such a belief is firmly entrenched, *any* alternative explanation is likely to be seen as preferable, as we shall see in chapter 6. Sadly, this was the case here. When Helen asked her father what he really thought about the event, he replied that she may never have had MS at all, and that the doctors had probably been wrong – 'After all, MS is very hard to diagnose.'

In New Testament times Jesus encountered similar attitudes. He was unable to do 'mighty works' in some places because of unbelief. Then, when he did perform miracles, some people attributed his power to cast out devils to the 'prince of devils'. Jesus pointed out the powerlessness of a kingdom undergoing civil war. This silenced his accusers, but left them unconvinced. Accusations like theirs are perilously close to the 'unforgivable sin' of attributing the works of God, through the Holy Spirit, to the devil.[2]

Questions, questions

An event of this kind raises a host of issues; this book attempts to tease out some of them. For instance:

● Prior to Helen's healing, her friends had prayed for some kind of direct action in her life. Was it any use their doing so? Did God, in the beginning, simply set everything going and leave it, or is he still active in the world? If he is active, how do believers reconcile this with his apparent inactivity, his apparent failure to heal or help? If God can heal and doesn't, what sort of a God does that make him?

● We use the word 'miracle' in all sorts of ways in everyday speech. But what does the Bible say about what miracles are? Why do miracles feature prominently in the Bible? Who does them? And when might they be expected nowadays?

● Helen had been educated in the mid-twentieth century, in an intellectual climate where science was popularly believed to have the ultimate say about what was or was not possible. Some people believed that science showed miracles could not happen, and that therefore they did not. But is this so? Questioning miracles 'in the name of science', however, is not new: the philosopher David Hume had done so in the eighteenth century, arguing that miracles contradicted the belief that nature always behaved uniformly. (This idea is known as the Uniformity of Nature.)

● Hume had also denied miracles on the grounds that the apparent 'witnesses' are unreliable. In the case of Helen's healing, the finger may seem to point accusingly in my direction, for so far you have only my word for this event. But it would be easy enough, at present, to produce others to corroborate my story, because witnesses are still alive. Fifty years on, however, when all the eyewitnesses are dead, there will probably be only this book and a few other documents to testify to the event. So people would need to research the answers to questions like, 'Is the author reliable?' and 'Has he correctly interpreted the events?' In other words, the evidence will be of an historical nature. In the same way, when we consider biblical miracles, historical evidence is crucial.

● One of the outstanding miracle-claims of the Bible is that God, the 'author' of the world's story, actually wrote himself into the 'play' and appeared 'on stage' at the Incarnation. So when Helen claimed to have experienced what can best be described as a 'personal encounter' with God, did she really 'meet the author'?

● Helen's story had a happy ending, but it might not have been so. Alongside the intellectual issues – if miracles do not happen, why don't they? If they do happen sometimes, why not more often? – lies a separate class of pastoral ones. Is there anything to be said when miracles don't happen, and it is your friend, child or parent who dies of cancer?

1 Helen's name, the names of her family and that of the town have been changed; the other details are correct.

2   Some people have worried about whether they have committed this sin, because it is said to be unforgivable. By way of reassurance, I would suggest that those who are worried have not committed it, since it is the continuing presence of the Holy Spirit that causes spiritual concern. The biblical passages seem to be talking about a persistent attitude of attributing the Holy Spirit's activities to Satanic powers.

2

Is God at work in the world?

Jane: I was desperate this morning. I had an interview at ten and two trains were cancelled. So I asked God to get me there on time, and just as I prayed my neighbour drew up and took me right to the door!

Mark: What a load of rubbish! God doesn't arrange things like lifts for you! He might look after the big things like keeping the seasons going, but that's all.

Colin: I don't think he even does that. He set everything going when he made the world, but it runs itself now. Things like your lift are just coincidences.

Stephen: You're all assuming there is a God. I don't believe there is one. This world is all there is.

Andrea: I think you're missing the point. God isn't some*body*; God is the whole world. When I look at a tree in blossom, or at a great mountain, I say, that's God!

Is God, as Jane thought, at work in the world? If so, in what way is he at work? These two questions are at the heart of the subject of miracles. When Helen's friends prayed for her healing, they clearly believed in God – not like Stephen, the *naturalist*, to whom the natural world was everything. Moreover, Helen's friends expected God to hear what they said, and to take some action – unlike Colin, the *deist*, who believed God had retired from the scene. Otherwise they would not have wasted their breath. They believed God was active in the world. But were they right to do so? If they were, in what way is God active? Did he just wind the world up when he made it and then leave it to carry on on its own, as Colin believed, or does he 'tinker with the works' to perform occasional miracles? Or is it that God and the world are one and the same thing, as *pantheists* like Andrea say? Perhaps God is like some slumbering giant, who has to be awakened by prayer and persuaded to 'intervene' in a world which he normally leaves to run on its own. Or maybe God's role is so reduced by scientific explanations, as one scientist claims, that

> . . . the creator had absolutely no job at all to do, and so might as well not have existed. We can track down the infinitely lazy creator, the creator totally free of any labour of creation, by resolving apparent complexities into simplicities, and I hope to find a way of expressing, at the end of the journey, how a non-existent creator can be allowed to evaporate into nothing and to disappear from the scene. (P Atkins *The Creation*, 1981, p 17, W H Freeman)

We can examine the 'infinitely lazy creator' view of God by seeing what it means to 'explain' – scientifically and otherwise – and by looking at the idea known as the 'god-of-the-gaps'. This we will do in the next chapter, but first we will look at the 'slumbering giant' view of God.

God as 'slumbering giant'?

We can explore this image of God's action in the world by looking at some of the beliefs of Colin the deist, Andrea the pantheist and Stephen the naturalist, and comparing their views with the Bible's view of God (biblical theism).

Colin's view: Deism

Deists like Colin credit God with the creation of the universe, but after that they regard him as the 'Retired Clockmaker'. Deism pictures God as powerful, but detached and remote, and considers it to be beneath God's dignity to 'tamper' with his creation once it is set up. A perfect machine, such as God would be expected to make, would not need adjustments. It was not that God *couldn't* 'interfere'; it was simply improbable that he *would*. So the picture presented by the deists is that of a God who, his work done, lets the universe run by itself, from the first 'tick' to the last 'tock'. Indeed, so little role is allowed to God that deism, in its extreme form, amounts to *atheism*.

Deism was particularly popular in the eighteenth century. It went along with the idea that there were unchanging natural laws, both physical and ethical, imposed upon the world by God. These laws were thought to be necessary, and to be discoverable by reason alone. Belief in the unchangability of these laws is apparent in this verse of an anonymous, eighteenth-century hymn:

Praise the Lord, for He hath spoken;
    Worlds His mighty voice obeyed;
Laws, that never shall be broken,
    For their guidance He hath made.

By this belief in natural laws, miracles were ruled out.

A more moderate form of deism took the view that God could perform occasional miracles in an otherwise clockwork world. Thus,

God was allowed, by most, to retain the key, and by the pious to hold a pair of tweezers by which to *intervene*. (R L F Boyd *Faith in this Space Age*, 1963, p 28)

17

According to this view, the world normally works by itself, without God's 'intervention' ('natural' behaviour). But occasionally God 'puts his oar in' and does miracles ('supernatural' behaviour). Some people see miracles as proofs of God, and attach importance to them for this reason. One problem with this view is that if miracles are not seen to be happening, there is no evidence of God's activity, and hence of God: what is ordinary is 'natural' and does not involve God; only what is miraculous is 'supernatural' and does involve God.

Stephen's view: Naturalism

Stephen the naturalist would also have agreed that what is ordinary is 'natural' and does not involve God. But for him it is only one step further to personify 'nature', and vest it with all the attributes formerly ascribed to God.

Thus Nature, spelt with a capital 'N', or even Mother Nature, will be spoken about as though it were an agent, controlling the whole world. (This does not make sense because Nature *is* the world!) Sometimes such talk seems little more than a metaphor, as when a meteorologist replied to an interviewer, after some unprecedented gales, 'Mother Nature played a card we didn't know she had'.

But a subtle form of conditioning arises from the persistent use of a seemingly innocuous figure of speech. For the word 'Nature' – which is not found in the Bible – has become a secular substitute for the word 'God'. The absurdity of denying God on the one hand, and elevating nature to a surrogate God on the other seems to pass unnoticed.

So the physical world is taken to be all there is, the source of its own being – whatever that means! This is *naturalism* and the view it takes is

a popular view that science shows nature to be running by itself according to a set of inviolable laws; and within this view lies the unwarranted philosophical assumption that a nature which runs according to a set of laws must also run by itself. (*Christian Graduate*, 25 (4), 1972, p 122)

To the naturalist, who has ruled out God from the beginning, *nothing* will act as evidence for miracles, since the category of 'miracle' is rejected from the start.

Andrea's view: Pantheism

Pantheists like Andrea say that God and the world are one and the same thing. So, unlike Stephen who uses the word 'nature' as though 'nature' were some kind of God, but *does not* believe it is, Andrea *does* believe it is and uses the words interchangeably.

The relationship between pantheism and science is an uneasy one. The ancient Greeks regarded nature as a semi-divine organism. So, performing experiments on 'her' seemed to them rather like sacrilege. This view of nature hindered experimental work during the period 600BC to AD200, with the result that Greek science gradually ground to a halt.

Perhaps you have found people with similar pantheistic ideas underlying their views of the environment. Pantheism is certainly characteristic of much 'New Age' thinking. Christians engaging with important environmental issues, need to be discerning, for it is not always easy to distinguish between responsible Christian management of the environment and an idolatrous 'reverence for nature'.

Pantheism seems to be associated with a current idea called the *Gaia hypothesis*, put forward by the scientist James Lovelock. According to this hypothesis, life shapes the environment, rather than the other way round. So far so good, for there is certainly a complex relationship between life and the environment, and the former does have effects on the latter. For example, many species of plankton in the sea produce a chemical which provides most of the condensation nuclei that encourage clouds to form over remote oceans. Some of the scientific claims of the Gaia hypothesis are contentious, but, even so, they *are* scientific questions, and can be tested scientifically.

However, Lovelock appears to be going further than merely talking about physical mechanisms. For he gives a name to the earth, calling it 'Gaia' after the name of the Greek earth goddess. He says, 'I see the world as a living organism of which we are a part.' It sounds rather like the ancient Greek world-view of the earth as an organism – especially in the hands of some of Lovelock's followers, who advertise themselves as being able to 'talk about Gaia from a mythological and theological point of view'.

The choice of a Greek goddess as a label for a set of scientific ideas introduces a cultic element. One scientist comments on the use of the name 'Gaia' as follows:

> . . . there is nothing in the Gaia metaphor that has not been utterly familiar to biologists for the whole of this century – except the name . . . That is why most biologists remained politely silent when, more than a decade ago, Lovelock indicated, in his engaging way, that he, too, had grasped these ideas. After all, when someone rediscovers the wheel, rather than say, 'I told you so', the more courteous of us nod with satisfaction that enlightenment has spread to yet another colleague and quietly get on with our business. But when the colleague proposes a Goddess of Wheeliness to unify the global aptness of his newly discovered wheel, we shake our heads sadly; and when Wheely-Goddess worshippers start popping up all over, then it is definitely time to worry. A principle of wheeliness, like a planet-sized organism, may be fun as imagery; as anything more scientific it is silly . . . Lovelock's scientific achievements are tremendous and deserve our respect. It is gratifying to all of us that

he found his Gaia metaphor stimulating and constructive. Let it remain a metaphor. (J Postgate, 'Gaia gets too big for her boots', *New Scientist*, 7 April 1988, p 60)

Biblical theism

The writers of the Bible share with deists a belief in God as creator of the universe. But they go further, saying that God is active moment by moment within his creation; that he is 'the upholder of all permanency and all change'. Contrary to the pantheist's assumption that God and the world are one and the same, the biblical view stresses the distinction between God and creation. It does not claim, however, as deism does, that God is completely detached from his work. The Bible's view of God affirms both the distinction between God and the world (known as God's transcendence), and also his total involvement with it (known as his immanence).

Against this background, a distinction between non-miraculous and miraculous, as being between the natural and the supernatural, can be seen to be potentially misleading. It misleads if it promotes the view that God is at work only in miraculous events – a view which has been evident in some recent Christian books about 'creation'. Some authors pepper their writings with claims concerning miracles in the early earth, far beyond any biblical warrant. It seems that unless particular events are physically inexplicable, such writers cannot see them as caused by God. There is a danger that this perception of God's ways of working can degenerate into a magical view of divine activity, reflecting a particular disposition within certain church traditions. It is no antidote to such a restricted view of God to say, 'Well, everything's miraculous, really.' That simply confuses different meanings of the word 'miracle'.

The 'natural', then, is the way God acts normally; on

special occasions he may act in a miraculous way.

> God acts, and if this action is repetitive and predictable we call it nature; if surprising or not within our current knowledge we call it a miracle. (E Ives *God in History*, 1979, p 26, Lion Publishing)

Psalm 135 makes this point clear: in verse 7 natural things, like clouds, rain and wind, are said to be God's activity, and, in the following verses, miracles such as Moses performed for Pharoah are attributed to God also.

God's total involvement in the world requires that miracles be recognised, not as evidence that God is acting where he does not normally act, but as indications that he is acting in ways, and for purposes, that are different from normal. In other words, it is the *mode*, not the *fact* of God's activity, that is different. In view of this, I think the labels 'ordinary' and 'extraordinary' would better describe the acts of God than 'natural' and 'supernatural'. According to the biblical view outlined above, therefore, Helen's healing was an extraordinary act of God in response to prayers of faith. It happened in connection with Tom's use of the Holy Spirit's gift of a 'word of knowledge'.

So if the biblical picture is of a God who, far from being a 'slumbering giant', is totally involved in the world, what can we discover about his activity? And how did the idea of an 'infinitely lazy creator' ever creep in? For answers to these questions we need a new chapter.

3

Active God or 'infinitely lazy creator'?

Alison: I think God's creation is fantastic!

David: I can't for the life of me see why you have to bring God into it. Didn't the French mathematician Laplace say, 'I have no need of that hypothesis'?

Neil: Since you ask, no he didn't! People say he did, but it's a legend for which there's no evidence whatsoever.

Tim: But the scientific explanation of creation is almost complete now – the gaps in our knowledge are closing fast, and there's precious little room left for God!

In the Bible God's action in the world is shown to be of three kinds: creating the world, sustaining it and redeeming it.

Creating the world
The agent of God's creative activity is shown, in a number of different New Testament passages, to be Jesus Christ. Three passages are of particular note.

The introduction to John's Gospel presents Christ as the Word of God:

> In the beginning was the Word, and the Word was with God, and the Word was God. He was with God in the beginning.
>
> Through him all things were made; without him nothing was made that has been made. (John 1:1–3)

In brief, this is saying that nothing exists except by Christ's doing. Sometimes this is expressed as *creatio ex nihilo* – creation out of nothing – although 'not out of anything' would be less open to misunderstanding.

The other two passages have three ideas in common: the *creation* of the world, the *sustaining* of the world and the *redemption* of the world:

> For by him [Christ] all things were created: things in heaven and on earth, visible and invisible, whether thrones or powers or rulers or authorities; all things were created by him and for him. He is before all things and in him all things hold together . . . For God was pleased to have all his fulness dwell in him, and through him to reconcile to himself all things, whether things on earth or things in heaven, by making peace through his blood, shed on the cross. (Colossians 1:16–20)

> In the past God spoke to our forefathers through the prophets at many times and in various ways, but in these last days he has spoken to us by his Son, whom he appointed heir of all things, and through whom he made the universe. The Son is the radiance of God's glory and the exact representation of his being, sustaining all things by his powerful word. After he had provided purification for sins, he sat down at the right hand of the Majesty in heaven. (Hebrews 1:1–3)

Sustaining the world

The creation of the world means its bringing-into-being-by-God. The sustaining of the world means its holding-in-being-by-God. If the world were not being sustained, there would not be chaos, but nothing. The kind of 'sustaining' being described, however, is a dynamic one, for the world is not static. At every level there is movement and change, from the stars down to the atoms.

It is impossible to find a comparison that is complex enough to illustrate this dynamic sustaining. We might make a comparison with a superhuman computer operator who projects each electron, individually, at the right place, speed and time, to make a moving computer graphics display. If the 'superbuff' ceased to act, it is not that the display would be distorted, it would simply cease to be. But like any model, this one has inadequacies. It is too deterministic, for it implies that everything is fixed in advance, by God. It fails to allow for the freedom of action of human agents to cause or to alleviate evil in a world that God created 'good'. But despite the inadequacies of the model, it serves to illustrate Christ's role as the Sustainer as well as the Creator, the Maintainer as well as the Maker, of the world.

Redeeming the world

Creation has a purpose, for God's intention is to 'bring all things in heaven and on earth together under one head, even Christ' (Ephesians 1:10). This purpose is not yet realised, for the entry of sin into the world has spoiled people's relationships with God, and it has also blighted the world itself, so that it is in urgent need of renewal:

> For the creation was subjected to frustration, not by its own choice, but by the will of the one who subjected it, in hope that the creation itself will be liberated from its bondage to decay and brought into the glorious freedom of the children of God.

> We know that the whole creation has been groaning as in the pains of childbirth right up to the present time. (Romans 8:20–22)

Human sin has affected the creation in at least two ways. People have brought suffering by doing what they *ought not* to have done and by failing to do what they *ought* to have done. Creation, even before the Fall, needed 'subduing'. It required responsible, but not exploitative, 'dominion'. People were to be the managers, not the owners. But loss of self-control resulted in loss of power to control creation. So, while such evils as malicious rumours and stab wounds are the results of *sins of commission*, some natural disasters may be the result of *sins of omission*.

A 'groaning' world, along with its unfaithful managers, needs redeeming if God's purpose of bringing 'all things in heaven and on earth together under one head' is to be realised. Hence the New Testament emphasis on Christ's threefold work as Creator, Sustainer and Redeemer.

The 'slumbering giant' picture of God's action (or lack of it) which we looked at in the last chapter, is a caricature of the biblical picture of God's total involvement with his world. Its restricted portrayal of God has something in common with another view referred to at the beginning of the last chapter, the infinitely lazy creator, 'totally free of any labour of creation'. He has been dubbed 'lazy' in the belief that scientific explanations replace what was formerly attributed to God, and so there is nothing left for him to do.

God as 'infinitely lazy creator'?

This odd notion seems to have arisen from imagining God as a kind of plug which can be pushed in, to fill the gaps in our scientific knowledge. On this view, if all the gaps in scientific knowledge were ever to be filled, God would become redundant, having nothing to do. But the idea is muddled because it treats 'God' as a *physical* explanation, *of the same type* as other physical explanations, filling the gaps in our scientific knowledge of the physical world. Rather, God is the author of the whole, both the parts we can explain scientifically, and those which, at present, we can not.

If this idea of a 'god-of-the-gaps' is accepted uncritically, people proceed from this point in different ways, depending upon whether they are pro- or anti-God.

A believer in God who falls for the 'god-of-the-gaps' idea may be wary of any filling of the gaps currently labelled 'God', since this will appear to decrease God's territory. And so science, which is filling gaps in knowledge all the time, is likely to be viewed by such a believer with suspicion, as not 'leaving room for God', and scientists, if not actually regarded as a godless lot, are likely to be eyed at least with caution — as I have found out!

The situation is different for the unbeliever. Obviously he does not believe in any God, gap-filling or otherwise. But he may believe that, if there were a God, he would be of the 'god-of-the-gaps' type. So the more scientific discoveries are made, the less 'room for God' there is. Science therefore appears to be a good stick with which to beat religion!

Actually, the fears of the believer and the hopes of the unbeliever are both unfounded. What Professor C A Coulson dubbed the 'god-of-the-gaps' is a theological and philosophical confusion.

It is a *theological* confusion because it is a caricature of the biblical portrayal of God as being involved in everything, not just the parts we happen to find puzzling at present.

It is a *philosophical* confusion because it substitutes explanations about the maker, which are of one type, with physical cause-and-effect explanations, which are of a different type, thus committing a *type-error* in explanation.

To illustrate this, imagine someone trying to understand one of James Watt's steam engines in the Science Museum. He sees that, when steam enters the cylinder, it pushes the piston up. But he cannot understand how the piston comes down again. 'Ah, that's Watt,' says his friend!

Of course, no sensible person would really substitute the inventor for an explanation of the mechanisms of the invention. The required answer to the gap in his knowledge of early steam engines is that cold water, sprayed on the cylinder, condenses the steam, and atmospheric pressure drives the piston down. The answer is not some kind of 'Watt-of-the-gaps'.

Although there are differences when the analogy is applied to God's activity, a similar point is being made. You don't fill gaps in scientific knowledge with talk-about-God, but by developing better scientific explanations.

There is a sense, not to be pressed too sharply, in which Watt *is* involved in the whole engine. It is his creation – both the bits we understand and the parts we do not. But if we dismantle the whole engine, down to the very last bolt, we don't suddenly come across Watt! Yet nonsense of a similar logical status is commonly talked about God.

The 'god-of-the-gaps' ensnares Christians and non-Christians alike, even though their reactions to it are opposite. But 'god-of-the-gaps' is only one of a whole family of muddles about the nature of explanations, scientific and otherwise, and a little more needs to be said about this.

Explaining – away?

There are two key misunderstandings about explanations commonly found in discussions about the origin of the universe and also on the issue of miracles:

- the view that there is only one *type* of explanation, a scientific one,

- the idea that to explain something scientifically, be it a miracle or the origins of the universe, is to explain it *away* from a theological point of view.

Some of the reasons why scientific explanations have been accorded such a high status are outlined in chapter 6, where we will also see why the reasons may be faulty. Scientific explanations are simply one type of explanation, and there is much discussion among philosophers as to what *is* a scientific explanation. One view is that an event has been explained scientifically if, given a universal law and the initial conditions, the event was predictable. This means that, given the laws of motion and gravity, it can be predicted where a given satellite will be at any given time, knowing its speed and position at some earlier time. Why the satellite is there has been *explained* scientifically.

But there are other possible explanations as to why the satellite is there, explanations of agency and purpose. Which nation put it into space? And for what purpose, peaceful or warlike? Clearly the presence of a satellite in space will have other types of explanations, which science cannot provide because it is restricted to explanations of the mechanisms. Nobody would be likely to claim that agency and purpose were 'explained away' by scientific explanations of the mechanisms. Yet, curiously, such an idea seems to gain currency as soon as the agent is said to be God – as can be seen from little asides slipped into some popular scientific books about the world's origins, asides like:

> It is now possible to give a good scientific answer to the question 'Where do we come from?' without invoking either God or special boundary conditions for the universe at the moment of creation. (J Gribbin *In Search of the Big Bang*, 1986, p 392, Bantam Books)

In view of what has been said about the god-of-the-gaps, this is strictly true; the scientific picture *is* becoming more complete. This sort of writing, however, leaves a misleading impression, that God is therefore pushed out of the picture – but this does not follow. Peter Atkins, in *The Creation*, is even more forthright:

> That such a universe as ours did emerge with exactly the right blend of forces may have the flavour of a miracle, and therefore seem to require some form of intervention [by God]. But nothing intrinsically lacks an explanation. We cannot yet see quite far enough to decide which is the right explanation, but we can be quite confident that intervention [by God] was not necessary. (pp 123, 5)

The confidence is misplaced. Science tells us nothing about First Causes, such as whether or not there is a God. Such matters lie outside its sphere of competence.

But now it is time to ask such questions as what is meant by 'miracles', and whether such things actually occur.

4

Talk about miracles

Janet: We prayed for someone with a brain tumour, and when he went to hospital for another scan there was no trace of it.

Maurice: That's just spontaneous remission. Miracles don't happen nowadays.

Gill: I don't think they ever did! Stories of miracles are just made up – or exaggerations about people getting better normally.

Sean: Well, I think miracles still happen. My mum climbed out unhurt after her car turned over three times when she was doing sixty! Wasn't that a miracle?

Many people with no religious convictions would call Helen's healing from MS 'a miracle'. And some of them would also say that it was a miracle to survive a parachute drop when the parachute didn't open, or, as Sean's mother did, to escape unscathed from a serious car crash.

'Wonder' is always an element of the miraculous. But does the biblical idea of miracle go further than that? And, if there are miracles, what exactly are they? Why do they happen? Who performs them, and when do they occur?

What are miracles?

The New Testament uses three main words for miracle:
- *dunamis*, an 'act of power'
- *teras*, a 'wonder'
- *semeion*, a 'sign'

Dunamis focuses attention on the *cause* of a miracle in the power of God. *Teras* refers to its *effect*, and *semeion* to its *purpose*. The two latter words are often used together. *Teras* is not applied to a miracle on its own. This may reflect the Bible's concern with the significance, rather than the spectacle, of miracles. In Acts 2:22 all three words are to be found:

> Jesus of Nazareth was a man accredited by God to you by miracles (*dunamis*), wonders (*teras*) and signs (*semeion*), which God did among you through him, as you yourselves know.

Old Testament words translated 'miracles' also mean signs and wonders.

Miracles in the Bible may be classified in various ways:
- those of nature, like Jesus' stilling of the storm on Lake Galilee (Mark 4:35–41);
- those specifically concerned with the healing of people's bodies, like the woman with a haemorrhage (Mark 5:25–34);
- those which involve the casting out of evil spirits, like the man whose name was 'Legion' (Mark 5:9–20);
- ones in which the miraculous element involves the timing of the event (Exodus 14:21f).

In some cases, more than one of these elements is present. There are detailed theological works which examine the types of miracle in detail.

For many people the major difficulty about miracles is a perceived tension with science, for science seems to assume the Uniformity of Nature, whereas miracles imply exceptions to this regularity. (It is, of course, only against a normal background of uniformity that miracles, as exceptions, have any meaning.) In this book, we shall focus on miracles as being events which are, in general, contrary to the normal behaviour of the natural world, described by scientific laws.

It is not easy to construct a neat definition of a miracle – even one which fits all those recorded in the Bible – as the following attempts show.

Something contrary to nature?

One early attempt at a definition was, 'a miracle is something which is contrary to nature'. Augustine (Bishop of Hippo in North Africa from AD 396–430) said this should be 'contrary to what is known of nature. For we give the name nature to the usual common course of nature.' One difficulty about 'contrary to nature' definitions is that what is currently thought to be 'contrary to nature' may turn out, with increasing knowledge, not to be so. The definition leans too heavily on our current level of understanding. For instance, how would the miracle of the crossing of the Red Sea, recorded in Exodus 14, fit that definition? A 'strong east wind' may be greater than usual, as were those that hit the British Isles in October 1987 and January 1990, but would we say that very strong winds were 'contrary to what is known of nature'?

The difficulty of knowing whether or not something is just a temporary anomaly, which will later fit into an enlarged scientific understanding, has triggered off a particular theological debate. Instead of concentrating on whether miracles are possible, the task has shifted to seeking criteria for recognising a miracle if we saw one.

The nature of explanation, reviewed in the last chapter, is relevant here. Can miracles be explained scientifically, and, if so, would this destroy their status? To some people, any explanation of a miracle would detract from it as an example of God's working; they feel that miracles must necessarily be shrouded in mystery. At the opposite end of the spectrum of personal preferences is the popular Victorian view of miracles that 'those that cannot be "explained" cannot be entertained'. The criterion of belief, for such people, is that a miracle must not stretch their imagination beyond the bounds of what seems possible from their current knowledge of the world!

But, in biblical thought, the fact that you cannot explain what has happened is neither a *necessary* nor a *sufficient* condition for an event to be a miracle. It is not a *necessary* one since, in the Red Sea narrative, an explanation *is* given. It is not a *sufficient* condition, since amazing things occur from time to time which, although not immediately explicable, do not have any particular theological significance.

Something that can be done only by God?

Another inadequate definition of 'miracle' is, 'an extraordinary operation performable by God alone'. This one overlooks the fact that, even in the Bible, not all miracles are attributed to God. The same deficiency is found in a recent definition: 'an extraordinary and striking event taken by the believer in God to be a special disclosure of His power and purpose.' This is hindered by an additional problem: what if God *intended* the event to be 'taken by the believer' as a sign, but the believer was too spiritually blind to see it? Perhaps the definition should be amended so as to replace the words 'taken by the believer in God' with 'intended by God'. Would that be any better?

The point I am moving towards is not so much that it is difficult to make watertight definitions, but that often it is not necessary to try to make them, despite the sense of security we may derive from them. Even in science it can be unwise to try to give a definition in answer to a question which starts 'Explain what is meant by a . . .'

You may have memories of starting to answer such

an examination question with 'A . . . is . . .', and finding yourself in grammatical confusion, unable to continue the sentence! Perhaps a more helpful way of proceeding is to forgo attempts at tidy definitions of miracles and to try instead to identify the essential features of a miracle. For simplicity, we will confine our attention to miracles performed by God.

Why miracles?

There appear to be two key features of a miracle.
• First, some striking event catches the attention.
• Second, the wonderful event is intended by God as a sign; it has theological significance.

Take for example the feeding of the 5,000 (plus women and children – John 6:5–59). It met an immediate need – satisfying the physical hunger of a spiritually 'hungry' crowd, who were so keen to hear Jesus that they followed him without thinking about their subsistence. But it was also significant in other ways. It was a sign that Jesus is Lord over creation and can order it as he wishes; it was an indication of his concern for everyday needs – he had compassion on the multitude. Its particular significance, however, as his subsequent words show, was as a vehicle for teaching that he, as the Bread of Life, could satisfy human spiritual 'hunger'.

Miracles play an integral part in the teaching and preaching of Jesus, as a sign that the Kingdom of Heaven (or the Kingdom of God) has drawn near. Jesus said, 'If I drive out demons by the finger of God, then the kingdom of God has come to you' (Luke 11:20). The King, Immanuel (God with us), walks his earth. The subduing of creation, with which humans were originally charged, is displayed as he stills the storm on Lake Galilee. His purpose in coming to destroy the works of the devil is exemplified by casting out demons. His love for individuals is shown in a variety of miraculous acts, (eg the restoring of sight to blind people), which bring comfort, healing and hope.

Finally, his power over the 'last enemy', death, is exhibited in the raising of Lazarus. Eventually, of course, Lazarus died again and he had no control over whether this would happen or not. So the supreme demonstration of the power of Jesus over death came with his own resurrection, a key event of Christianity. For when Jesus rose, it was not to die again; he rose to the power of an endless life. This event, as well as his death, was very much under his control: 'I have authority to lay [my life] down and authority to take it up again' (John 10:18).

Although miracles are presented as integral to Jesus' ministry, they are not given as 'knock-down proofs' of his divinity, from which the sceptic has no escape. As Francis Bacon, the English statesman and philosopher of science, put it,

> God never wrought miracles to convince atheism,
> because his ordinary works convince it.

So it is only in a general way that miracles authenticate the messenger of God and testify to the truth of the message. For Scripture recognises, and warns, that 'false Christs and false prophets will appear and perform signs and miracles to deceive the elect – if that were possible' (Mark 13:22).

Who performs miracles?

Since biblical miracles are attributed to powers other than God – as with the activities of Pharaoh's magicians in the Old Testament and those of Simon the Sorceror in the New – miracles cannot be taken as proofs of God. There are, however, differences between the miracles of God and those coming from other sources, for the Bible does not teach dualism – equal and opposite powers of good and evil struggling for supremacy. The magicians of Pharaoh were limited in their powers and unable to replicate some of the miracles that Moses did. A major difference between the miracles of Jesus and those that 'could be witnessed in any Egyptian marketplace' was pointed out by Origen (c AD 185–254):

> ... no sorcerer uses his tricks to call spectators to moral reformation; nor does he educate by the fear of God people who were astounded by what they saw, nor does he attempt to persuade the onlookers to live as men who will be judged by God. Sorcerers do none of these things, since they have neither the ability nor even the will to do so.

Miracles of God accompany kingdom-of-God activity; and Jesus sent his disciples to preach, 'the kingdom of God is near you', with power to heal the sick and cast out demons. Since this is exciting work, Jesus cautioned the jubilant disciples, when they returned in a state of euphoria, that the ground of their permanent rejoicing should be 'that your names are written in heaven' (Luke 10:20).

Miracles – past, or present too?

A contentious issue within the church continues to be whether the power to work signs and wonders was given only at certain times in the Old Testament and to the early church, or whether it remains part of the equipment available for Christians today. In discussing the issue it is important to distinguish between assertions and arguments. An assertion tells us what someone believes, but it gains no more weight through constant repetition. It prepares us to listen to supporting arguments, but it is not itself an argument.

It was this issue that Helen's father and his fellow elders had struggled with. Their conclusion, which followed in a long line of church tradition, went something like this: 'Miracles are not for today. They were only necessary to establish the early church and then they disappeared.'

The first sentence is a simple *assertion*, like the common Victorian one, 'miracles do not happen'; it expresses a conviction, but gives no supporting argument. The second sentence offers two further assertions, support for which is usually sought from 1 Corinthians 13:8–10:

> Love never fails. But where there are prophecies, they will cease; where there are tongues, they will be stilled; where there is knowledge, it will pass away. For we know in part and we prophesy in part, but when perfection comes, the imperfect disappears.

The reasoning goes something like this: Paul, writing in the first century AD said that prophecies would cease, tongues would be stilled and knowledge would pass away. Since 'we know in part and we prophesy in part', these things are imperfect and they disappear 'when perfection comes'. But perfection *has* come in the written Word of God, as the Scriptures were completed. So the imperfect has disappeared and spiritual gifts, which include 'prophecies', 'tongues' and 'miraculous powers', are not for the church today.

The argument hinges on identifying 'when perfection comes' as being the completion of the New Testament and, broken down into its parts, it goes like this:

1 Scripture is divinely inspired
2 therefore it is perfect
3 'perfection' in Paul's letter must therefore refer to the Scriptures
4 'perfection comes' must therefore refer to the completion of the Scriptures.

There is no need to make any alterations to 1 or 2 in order to point out the invalidity of arguing 'Scripture is perfect, therefore "perfection" must refer to the Scriptures'. A trivial statement, set out in similar form, may make the fallacy clear: 'Apples are fruit, therefore "fruitiness" must refer to apples.'

The 'therefore' is misplaced. 'Fruitiness' *can* refer to apples, but it is not exclusive to them. It can also apply to pears, plums and pomegranates. The claim that 'when perfection comes' must mean the completion of the Scriptures, is like insisting that 'when happiness comes' must mean 'the completion of this book', just because I shall feel happy to have finished writing it. But happiness might also refer to my going on holiday or being given an unexpected present. Although happiness *may* be associated with the completion of the book, and perfection *may* be linked with the completion of the Scriptures, the first does not entail the second in either case. Indeed, without additional information, there is no way in which someone, given the first, could deduce the second. So it is difficult to see how a convincing argument for the cessation of miracles and other spiritual gifts can be mounted from this passage of Scripture.

But the claim that 'miracles are not for today' has been argued for in another way, by saying, 'as a matter of fact we don't see miracles like those New Testament ones today, so they must have ceased'. One cannot truthfully deny that those who argue in this vein probably never have seen miracles themselves, but obviously it will not do to say, 'I have never seen a miracle, so miracles do not happen'. We must take into account that miracles, by their very nature, are unusual. Nevertheless, there are innumerable reports, stretching down the centuries, of miraculous events. In our own time, especially since the charismatic renewal, there are witnesses to miraculous healings. No doubt some reports – perhaps many – are spurious, and some come through wishful thinking; in some cases people are simply deluded – for Christians, too, can be gullible about what they want to believe. But we cannot with integrity write off the residue of testimonies which come from sane and balanced people drawn from all walks of life, people whose testimonies would be accepted in a court of law. To do so would expose an individual prejudice that *no* evidence would be sufficient to support miraculous claims, a prejudice which will be examined in chapter 7.

Only one miracle is needed to falsify the assertion 'miracles do not happen'.

Certainly the Bible records miraculous claims as being more frequent at some times than others. Three main periods were:

- the times of Moses and Joshua (14th–13th centuries BC)
- the times of the 9th-century prophets, Elijah and Elisha
- New Testament times

But the absence of large numbers of recorded instances of miracles is not a sufficient reason for inferring their demise. Other possible explanations include one furnished by Jesus himself: 'he did not do many miracles there because of their lack of faith' (Matthew 13:58).

In conclusion, the preceding arguments for the cessation of miracles appear to me to be deficient. There seem to be good grounds in the New Testament for expecting miracles still to accompany the preaching of the gospel, as a means of convincing people that the power of God is still at work today.

5

Whatever do they teach them at school?

Dad: When I was your age, our science teacher made us remember lots of facts for exams. 'Science *is* facts,' he used to tell us. He hadn't much time for religion: 'That's faith', he would say, 'and you can't prove it. But science proves things; give me the facts any day.'

Sarah: That's old hat, Dad. In the National Curriculum we get taught that there are processes and skills in science, as well as facts. We also get told about the limited nature of proof and that science isn't the only way of looking at the world.

Jonathan: Yes, my science teacher tells us that too. She says the way science works isn't quite as simple as people used to think, because our own ideas influence which facts we take into account. She's religious, too, not like your old science teacher!

Mum: I wish I'd been taught science nowadays, not the way we used to be taught. I'm not particularly religious but people seemed to treat science a bit like a God, having the last word on everything.

People's views of science change, as do the ways in which philosophers view the scientific enterprise. But the public's views lag behind those of the philosophers and there has been a similar lag, until recently, in the way science teachers have taught about the nature of science. In recent years the public understanding of science has been considered so important that the Royal Society set up a small group to investigate ways in which it could be improved. The group's recommendations were published in *The Public Understanding of Science* (1985). In the 1980s, also, the first Chair in the Public Understanding of Science was established, in the University of London.

In the 1950s, when Helen was being educated, the particular pattern of science education current at that time would have moulded her formal learning in science, and her informal learning would have been shaped by current popular thought about the nature and status of science. When the possibility of miracles attracted her attention later on, these earlier inputs would have influenced her expectations.

Helen's science education

Science education in the 1950s was largely a matter of transmitting received knowledge to the next generation. Of course, good teachers have always encouraged their pupils to question and think for themselves, but much of the science education of the mid-century was little more than the learning of facts for examinations. It was supported by a style of practical work which set out to 'prove' known facts and laws by standard experiments, under such headings as Aim, Apparatus, Method, Results and Conclusion.

Little attention was given to helping pupils appreciate the nature of the scientific enterprise – its limitations, as well as its strengths. Graduate science teachers generally received no instruction in the history and philosophy of science in their first degree science courses – a situation which is little improved today. Non-graduate teachers, similarly, were ill-prepared to teach the nature of science, as distinct from its content. A decade would pass before the first Nuffield teaching schemes began to move science teaching away from rote learning. The re-emphasis of those schemes on discovery learning was to spark off an unprecedented wave of science curriculum reform, culminating in Science and Technology as set out in the National Curriculum.

The implicit understanding that would have been conveyed to Helen was that science meant certainty. It was a body of facts arrived at by the so-called Scientific Method. This supposed Method, slightly caricatured, was thought to start with the collection of data without preconceived notions, followed by induction – the making up of general laws from specific instances.

Changing attitudes to science

Charles Coulson, the first Professor of Theoretical Physics at King's College London, often made the point that much of the blame for the tensions which were still being felt between science and religion must be laid on bad science education. Sir Robert Boyd, Professor of Physics at University College London and Director of the Mullard Space Research Laboratory, echoed this view when he referred to the responsibility of the science educator:

> Those of us who are in any way concerned with science, education or the press have an iconoclastic [breaking images or idols] responsibility. The popular image of science must be broken and science must be seen for what it is, an important cultural activity, perhaps the most important, nevertheless an activity made, like the sabbath, for man, not man for science. I believe that no small part of the cynicism and scepticism and the lack of any sense of purpose or any genuine faith, which affects a section of youth today,

is due to the erroneous view of science that many of them have received from their school teachers. It seems to me to be vitally important that those who will teach our young people in the future must themselves have been taught not only science, but sufficient of the history and philosophy of science to prevent them presenting the image of a false god to their pupils. (*Faith in this Space Age*, 2nd Rendle Short Memorial Lecture)

The date of these words is particularly interesting. They were spoken at a public lecture in 1963, at about the time Helen was receiving her secondary education. But the quarter century that followed saw little change in popular views concerning the supposed conflict between science and religion.

The history of science has uncovered the power struggles, and sometimes the plottings, which have generated the popular legend of science and religion being at war. The warfare model never was a true picture. It is even less credible today. In the nineteenth century tensions were exaggerated in the interest of controversy, and deliberate and successful attempts were made to propagate the idea of conflict. This was to further the struggle for cultural supremacy, in which many scientists were involved. (See C A Russell, 'The Conflict Metaphor and its Social Origins' in *Science and Christian Belief*, 1989, **1**(1) pp 3–26.)

Popular thinking about science

Helen would have been influenced not only by the 'hidden curriculum', in science lessons, of an inflated view of the role of science, but also by the 'received wisdom', the public perception, concerning the nature of science. Another public lecture, also given at the time of Helen's secondary education, summed up what was then continuing to be the popular understanding of science:

In popular misconception, science is believed to be omnipotent: what it has not yet achieved it will ultimately achieve. It is believed to be infallible; to say of anything, that it is scientific, is thought to give it the impress of truth, the certainty which brooks no shadow of doubt. Even the packets of breakfast cereals bear witness to this; advertisement owes much of its power to the weight carried by a so-called scientific statement; to attribute scientific qualities to some process or other is to stifle criticism. Naturally, the advertiser allows no hint of uncertainty to mar his claims when he dubs them scientific; hence they become indisputable, eternally true, profoundly significant – at least they do in the eyes of those susceptible to the wiles of advertising. The television screen and the loudspeaker are as blatant and even more clamorous. Popular journalism preaches the same gospel: science is certainty; the findings of a research team must be true; mistakes are never made; progress is uninterrupted. (A M Taylor *Imagination and the Growth of Science*, 1966, pp 3f, John Murray)

Helen's awakening interest

Against this background, and the widespread view that science had displaced religion, Helen might have been expected to have had a predisposition against miracles!

In fact, she had become a Christian a few years before she went to secondary school. She encountered opposition to miracles largely in her religious education, from a geography teacher who took some religious education as a sideline. He taught Helen for several years and made it quite clear he did not believe in miracles.

Helen's first encounter with miraculous healing followed the sudden illness of her first child. Sarah contracted meningitis through a visit to a swimming pool and her case was diagnosed as hopeless. The doctor said she was unlikely to live and that if she did she would almost certainly be a 'vegetable'. But the doctor concerned was a Christian and said he would pray for the little girl. Exciting things began to happen. The local newspaper carried the following report which, although sensationalised, is substantially true:

' "Lifetime" coma girl wakes up', 'Daughter saved by "miracle cure" claims mother', 'NO MEDICAL REASON'

'For three weeks, eight-year-old Sarah Johnson lay paralysed and deeply unconscious in a hospital bed.

She had cerebral thrombosis, and doctors told her mother that she might stay in a coma for the rest of her life.

But then a "miracle" happened – and yesterday Sarah was cycling around her home . . . as if nothing had happened.

Her recovery amazed doctors and surgeons . . .

Despite brain surgery and electro-impulse treatment, Sarah did not respond and specialists warned her mother.

Said Mrs Johnson: "Then the congregation at my evangelical church organised a chain of prayer throughout all our churches.

"After three weeks in a coma, she suddenly opened her eyes and spoke to a nurse.

"Soon she was as right as rain and able to come home. We hardly dared believe that a miracle could happen." '

Miracles under review

The report, in its readable journalese, stands in contrast to a much more sober newspaper insert which appeared in *The Times* on 13 July 1984, signed by a group of distinguished scientists and indicating their belief in miracles. It attracted attention, and an editorial, in the prestigious journal, *Nature*, ran as follows:

> The presidents of the Linnean Society and of the Bible
> Creation Society of the United Kingdom, Dr Sam
> Berry [Professor of Genetics] and Mr E H Andrews
> [Professor of Materials Science], together with a vice-
> chancellor, a fellow of the Royal Society and other
> worthies, last week startled readers of the London
> *Times* by intervening in a theological dispute which
> has riven the Anglican community in Britain – the
> propriety of installing as Bishop of Durham a man
> who professes himself (on television) to have an open
> mind on questions such as the Virgin Birth and the
> Resurrection. Briefly, the Linnean president and his
> fellow-believers say, 'it is not logically valid to use
> science as an argument against miracles'.

A lively correspondence followed, in which scepticism and
belief were both expressed (some of the issues arising
from the Bishop of Durham's views about miracles are
examined in the appendix). Two years later, when differences of interpretation within the Church of England were
giving rise to a re-examination of biblical miracles, *Nature*
published (24 July 1986) a detailed defence of miracles by
Professor Berry under the title, *What to believe about
miracles.*

In the public perception of science, two main strands of
thought are to be found. Much of the earlier triumphalist
view about the nature of science is still evident, and advertisers continue to use 'science' and 'scientific' as prestige
words to attract customers. But alongside the veneration
of science there co-exists a measure of distrust in both
science and technology. This is reflected in some aspects
of the Green movements. Instead of science and technology being viewed as unsullied benefactors, sorting out
our problems and giving us a better standard of living,
they are now themselves being seen as part of the problem.
Nevertheless, many people who think this way also believe

that science and technology will solve the problems they have created.

Changing patterns in science education

There has been a move away from a content-dominated curriculum to one which emphasises the skills and processes of science, and also gives consideration to its nature and its interactions with society. The National Curriculum for Science now requires that:

> Pupils should be given opportunities to develop their knowledge and understanding of how scientific ideas change through time and how their nature and the use to which they are put are affected by the social, moral, spiritual and cultural contexts in which they are developed. In doing so they should begin to recognise that, while science is an important way of thinking about experience, it is not the only way.

The role of beliefs and values also receives attention in Technology in the National Curriculum. Such changes are recent ones and will take time to affect the national consciousness, but they are to be welcomed.

Now, having taken a brief look at how science is presented and perceived, it is time to enquire more closely into the nature of science and to see what light, if any, this throws on the matter of miracles.

6

Hasn't science disproved miracles?

Charles: Science is the key to the world. It's only a matter of time before science unlocks all the secrets of the universe. That'll show how silly people are who believe in God and miracles and things like that.

Sue: You're right! Scientific laws make miracles and all that kind of stuff impossible.

Barry: But I thought scientific laws were about what *did* happen, rather than saying what *couldn't happen.*

There have been changes in the public perception of science, and there have also been changes in the ways philosophers of science have come to see it. So, in order to understand better the relationship between science and miracles, it would be useful to see how science came to have such a high status – as in Charles' view – at the middle of this century, and how the views held by philosophers of science have changed since then.

What follows is a whistle-stop tour of a selection of key ideas that have shaped current thinking about science. This will demonstrate some of the radical re-appraisal that has taken place, a re-appraisal that promises a more congenial relationship between science and religion.

Towards the end of the nineteenth century, science was seen as certain, the supreme example of knowledge. Matter was viewed as indestructible and the world as deterministic – meaning that, for everything that happens, conditions are such that nothing else could happen. In the view of the French astronomer, Laplace, the only obstacle to a complete knowledge of what would happen was our ignorance of its exact state at any particular moment. But given the initial conditions and the laws, the future appeared to be predictable in principle. Laplace imagined a superhuman intelligence which could know the position of, and the forces on, every particle in the universe at a particular time. To such an intelligence, he said, 'nothing would be uncertain and the future, as the past, would be present to its eyes'. Or, to move from philosophy to poetry, in the words of Edward Fitzgerald:

> Yea, the first Morning of Creation wrote
> What the Last Dawn of Reckoning shall read.

This couplet, from the *Rubaiyat of Omar Khayyam*, captures the fatalism that accompanies a deterministic view of the world. In this view there appears to be an inevitability about the world; freewill seems to be an illusion and human responsibility a deception.

Scientific laws

At times even the laws of science seem to be credited with the almost magical power of 'determining' the behaviour of the world, instead of being recognised as simply concise descriptions of the world's normal courses of action. As the rationalistic idea of 'law' as 'necessity' went out of favour, there was a shift away from the belief that miracles were impossible to the belief that they simply did not happen – 'miracles cannot happen' came to be replaced by 'miracles do not happen'.

The use of the word 'law' in connection with science has often caused problems over miracles – as it did with Sue at the beginning of the chapter – because miracles seem to 'break' the laws. The introduction of the word 'laws' in science seems to have arisen by analogy with the laws that regulate societies. Since laws in society give rise to order in society, the order that scientists find in the world might be thought of as involving 'laws' as well. But there is potential confusion in using the word 'law' in two such different ways.

Scientific laws are concise generalisations concerning the normal course of nature. The process of making them up has been compared to map-making. If new data come along which do not fit the scientific laws, then it is the laws, like the maps, which need changing. But even so, it is only new data of the *normal* kind that necessitate modifying laws and maps. A miracle is a unique event and demands no changes in scientific laws.

Charles Kingsley called the laws of nature, the 'customs of God', the ways God normally acts. But God is not bound never to depart from these regular patterns. If he wishes to act differently, on particular occasions for particular purposes, that is up to him. It is his world, to order as he wishes. Scientific laws are our attempts to express in a concise way the normal patterns of the world's behaviour.

Laws of the land may be 'broken' or 'obeyed'. These same two words are sometimes used in connection with scientific laws, but they are mis-used if borrowed and employed in this way. Scientific laws can be neither 'broken' nor 'obeyed', and events can only be 'in accordance with' or 'not in accordance with' scientific laws.

Another word that is borrowed from the legal world is 'govern'. Because laws of the land are used to govern a country, scientific laws are sometimes confusingly said to 'govern' events. But they do no such thing; they only describe them. They no more govern events than the contour lines on a map 'govern' where the mountain top shall be. To talk in this way about scientific laws 'governing', is the tail wagging the dog. Unfortunately such expressions get used so frequently that they gain 'squatter's rights' and their implications are difficult to dislodge.

Similarly, laws may be spoken of as if they made things happen. 'So [one scientist] speculates that the laws of physics started with absolutely nothing and created our universe out of the void. God was not involved in the Creation,' wrote Max Whitby in *The Listener* (8 March 1984, p 10, 'Our universe was created out of the void'.) C S Lewis's comment on this kind of talk stands in stark contrast:

> The dazzlingly obvious conclusion now arose in my mind: *in the whole history of the universe the laws of nature have never produced a single event* . . . The *laws* are the pattern to which events conform: the source of events must be sought elsewhere. (C S Lewis 'The Laws of Nature' in *God in the Dock*, 1979, p 53, Collins)

The difference between the two meanings of the word 'law' is sometimes expressed by saying that the laws of the land are *prescriptive*, while scientific laws are *descriptive*. This is quite a helpful distinction, but it is unwise to press it too far. For there *is* a way in which scientific laws may be said to be prescriptive: they prescribe, not what is *possible*, but what is *to be expected* on the basis of precedent. What has happened before indicates to us what we should normally expect to happen next time. The word 'normally' is the key word. So, because scientific laws are concise descriptions of normal patterns of behaviour, 'belief in miracle does not destroy the "integrity" of the scientific methodology, but only its "sovereignty" '.

Snared by success?
As time went on, the growing achievements of science bred

a confidence in its supposed 'Method' and its findings. It seemed that anyone could go out and collect the facts – which were there for all to see – and arrive at the same conclusions. Science seemed the perfect example of objectivity. Consensus generated a sense of certainty, in contrast to the subjective judgments involved in the arts, and particularly in religion. Because science draws directly on the evidence of the senses, it seemed that one could be certain in science, *positive* of its 'assured results'. This confidence – or overconfidence – led to a view of science called Positivism. The word came from the idea of something about which one could be positive, something given or laid down which just has to be accepted as we find it. It refers to the positive acquisition of knowledge through the senses. The main claims of positivism are that science is the only valid knowledge and that facts are the only possible objects of knowledge. Consequently, it denies the existence or intelligibility of anything that goes beyond facts and the laws formulated in science, and so is opposed to metaphysics – attempts to explain reality as a whole – and to religion. Positivism is encapsulated in the closing words of Bertrand Russell's book, published back in 1935, entitled *Religion and Science*:

> Whatever knowledge is attainable, must be attained by scientific methods; and what science cannot discover, mankind cannot know.

However, within science itself, revolutionary changes began to occur which were to challenge and finally overthrow this view of science, although for a time a rather triumphalist image continued to develop and strengthen. What was of particular significance for debates about science and religion was that the positivist view of science was taken up by a group of philosophers in Vienna (the Vienna Circle) during the 1920s and 30s, and developed into a full-blown theory about what could meaningfully be said about anything. The theory was known as Logical Positivism.

Logical positivism

The word 'positivism', as used about science, was joined with the word 'logical' because the theory was to do with *meaning*, and was considered to follow from science as a matter of logic. The analysis which follows now is a little more technical than the rest of this chapter. But it would be helpful to be aware of the claims and the weaknesses of logical positivism in order to understand its influence on popular thought, and how it has affected ideas about the relationship between science and religion.

The Vienna Circle took the view that the method of philosophy was not different from that of science. For them the task of philosophy was to find those principles that were common to all the sciences and to apply them as guides in human conduct and social structures. The logical positivists embodied their thinking in the famous 'Verification Principle': 'The meaning of a proposition is the method of its verification.' (A proposition is a technical term for a saying such as 'the sky is blue', which can be agreed with or denied.)

The logical positivists used the philosopher Hume's separation between analytic and empirical (or synthetic) truths, and claimed that there are only two classes of meaningful propositions.

First, there are *analytic* propositions, which are agreements, such as definitions, about how we will use words. 'A boy is a male child' is an analytic proposition. It is a tautology. It answers the question, 'What is a boy?' The converse question, 'What is a male child?' is answered by, 'A boy'. There is no way of making an experimental test of the truth of this answer. Analytic propositions tell us nothing about how things are in the world, only about how we agree to use words.

Second, there are *synthetic* propositions which can be

shown to be true or false by appealing to sense data. They are so called because they synthesise, or put together, claims about the world which can be put to experimental (empirical) test. 'That boy is a metre tall' is a synthetic proposition, because it brings together the idea of a boy and the concept of height. So it imparts new knowledge about the world, which may be tested.

Analytic and synthetic propositions were the only ones allowed by the Vienna Circle to have meaning. Any other propositions, such as 'God is love', they counted as meaningless, because they were not open to direct sensory tests. Equally meaningless, according to their criterion, was the atheist's proposition, 'God does not exist'.

Logical positivism provided a polite way of dismissing metaphysics and religion. It did not say that religious claims were not true, just that they had no meaning and were, technically, non-sense. It stopped short of discussing their truth, since questions of meaning are logically prior to questions of truth. If something has no meaning, it is pointless trying to decide whether it is true or not. To illustrate this point, take these lines by Lewis Carroll:

'Twas brillig, and the slithy toves
   Did gyre and gimble in the wabe:

Before you can usefully discuss the *truth* of the proposition 'the slithy toves did gyre and gimble', you have to decide whether it has any *meaning*.

A J Ayers' 'English manifesto of logical positivism', *Language, Truth and Logic*, published in 1936 (the year after Russell's *Religion and Science*), fell on ready ears, even though, in 1934, the weakness of logical positivism had already been indicated by Sir Karl Popper in the German version of his *Logic of Scientific Discovery*. Popper pointed out that the emphasis placed on 'verification' by the logical positivists was off-target, because no amount of supportive data can verify something up to the hilt. Unknown exceptions are always a possibility.

Logical positivism quickly ran into a host of difficulties. It appeared to be self-destructing. For, as was soon pointed out, the much vaunted Verification Principle was itself neither analytic nor synthetic – so it should be meaningless! Also, science involves a lot of assumptions – such as the Uniformity of Nature – which cannot be verified. So science, on which the whole superstructure of logical positivism was claimed to be based, fell an early victim of the very criterion of meaning that the logical positivists had themselves laid down!

To try to answer the criticisms, the Verification Principle was weakened in its claims. More recently it has come under heavy criticism for its ideas of theory-independent facts and its failure to recognise the role of models in scientific explanation.

Although logical positivism is now largely dead among professional philosophers, its ghost tends to live on as a way of thinking among scientists and, more especially, in popular thinking. It is this ghost which prompts such popular demands as 'prove to me scientifically that God exists', a demand which assumes that the methods of science are appropriate for all modes of enquiry, including religious ones.

Following this episode, developments in the philosophy of language highlighted the weaknesses of theories about the meaning of language based upon so-called scientific principles. Emphasis was laid on the importance of looking at the way language is used, rather than laying down stipulations about its meaning in advance.

Constant change is here to stay

From the end of the nineteenth century, everything seemed to be changing in science. The next few pages detail some of these changes, in order to show how over-confidence about science was challenged by fresh insights. As Stephen Leacock remarked, 'It was Einstein who made the real trouble. He announced in 1905 that there was no such thing as absolute rest. After that there never was.' But that is jumping ahead a little.

In America, in 1892, Professor Michelson summed up what he saw as the state of physics at the time:

> While it is never safe to affirm that the future of Physical Science has no marvels in store even more astonishing than those of the past, it seems probable that most of the grand underlying principles have been firmly established, and that further advances are to be sought chiefly in the rigorous application of these principles to all the phenomena which come under our notice...
>
> An eminent physicist has remarked that the future truths of Physical Science are to be looked for in the sixth place of decimals.

But what surprises there were in store!

In 1895 X-rays were discovered and, a few months later, in 1896, radioactivity. In 1897 the existence of electrons was established. No longer could atoms be thought of as 'un-cut-uppable' as their name implies. It seemed that elements could even change into other elements – something that was eventually to provide a 'clock' for dating the world. It wasn't quite the philosopher's stone, turning all to gold, though it might sound like it. But even the making of gold from another element was eventually found to be possible – by neutron bombardment – even if it was at considerably greater expense than buying gold over the counter!

The year that marked the twentieth century also marked the beginnings of quantum theory. It came about because of the total failure of one, rather dry-sounding experiment to fit in with current theory about energy. It led Max Planck, a German physicist, to suggest an entirely new way of looking at energy. He said that it must be thought of as coming in fixed-sized packets, or *quanta*, not in continuous streams.

Quantum theory was born and, like many new ideas, it was strongly resisted, although it was eventually to revolutionise physics. The idea might not have been taken up so quickly had it not been for the support of a young clerk in a Swiss patent office. He used quantum ideas to explain the kind of behaviour we sometimes use in photo-electric exposure meters. He developed a 'photo-electric equation' and was awarded a Nobel prize for his work. Not content with that achievement, Einstein – for that was his name – made another dramatic contribution in that same year of 1905. He put forward his famous Theory of Special Relativity, a theory which occasioned the earlier remark about 'absolute rest'!

Newton's ideas of absolute space and time were gone, to be replaced by 'spacetime'. If quantum theory seemed curious, special relativity seemed positively bizarre – time slowing down, distances contracting and bodies getting more massive near the speed of light. It was a science-fiction writer's paradise. But the old absolutes of space and time which disappeared were to be replaced by a new absolute – the velocity of light. It didn't matter how or where you measured it, it was always the same and it was an ultimate limit on how fast you could go.

This latter point about a new absolute is sometimes overlooked. I was once introduced as a physicist to a churchgoer at a party. Unaware of my Christian beliefs, he responded with jocular mistrust for, he said, he believed in absolutes, whereas presumably I believed all was relative on account of Einstein. I soon disabused him of his supposition that relativity in physics entailed relativism in religion and morals. This is a philosophical mistake: it does not.

In 1916 Einstein put forward his General Theory of Relativity, which was a new theory of gravitation involving the curvature of spacetime, the bending of light in strong gravitational fields and the prediction of Black Holes.

Then in 1927 a German physicist, Heisenberg, threw down the gauntlet to determinism in his famous Principle of Indeterminacy, by saying that some knowledge is for ever denied to us, because the act of trying to gain it would change what we were trying to find out. The idea, which has its most noticeable effect with tiny 'particles', like electrons, might be compared with a blindfolded person trying to find the position of a football by walking about, swinging his leg, on an otherwise empty football pitch. When he finally locates the ball, it isn't in the place that it would have been if he hadn't been looking for it. The attempt to find its position has altered it.

Changing views of the nature of science

In the philosophy of science, as well as in science itself, radical changes were taking place. The belief that science verified things beyond doubt was being challenged. Sir Karl Popper (in 1934) had pointed out that no number of experiments is sufficient to prove something beyond doubt. You cannot arrive at universal laws from particular instances; however many white swans are found, this does not justify the universal statement, 'all swans are white'. This is the so-called Problem of Induction. You have only to find one black swan to disprove, or falsify, the statement. So, said Popper, the emphasis in science should be on falsification, not verification. For although a general law cannot be proved up to the hilt, one counter-example will falsify it.

Part of the problem over the idea of 'proving' has arisen from the way the meaning of 'proof' has changed over the years. Its archaic meaning was 'to test', 'to try out', with the sense of ap*proving*. Even today the word is sometimes used in this way, as in a rocket 'proving' ground. But in common speech, to 'prove' has come to mean 'to show beyond any shadow of doubt'. This is impossible in almost every walk of life, apart from formal logic and some branches of mathematics. There are always questions that may be asked.

Science is seen nowadays to be a very different activity from the depersonalised processing of facts into universal laws by the turning of a handle marked 'The Scientific Method'. Creativity plays its part, as do lucky hunches. Our existing ideas and theories affect what we look for and what we select as important. For example, nobody performing experiments on floating objects would bother to consider whether the objects were made in Germany or Wales, nor whether their colours were attractive or not. These factors are unconsciously selected out by prior theories. Cultural factors play a part, too. As in religion, the use of metaphors, analogies and models are found to play a key role.

The social and moral dimensions of the scientist's activity are increasingly recognised, giving the lie to the notion of the scientist being able to shelter from responsibility by saying, 'I make the discoveries; it's up to you how you use them.' The historical dimension of the growth of science has attracted attention, and recent work in history of science has highlighted the important contribution of religion to the development of science in the West. The arrogant view of science as the final test of everything that we believe has been found to be inadequate, and it is now seen that there are good reasons for exercising a spirit of humility about the nature of science.

But in any discussion of science and religion, it needs constantly to be remembered that scientists, science teachers and philosophers are people. Personal predispositions – and we all have them – powerfully affect what we expect and what we 'see', as will again be apparent in the next chapter.

7

Thinking about miracles

Samantha: However much evidence you said you could produce for a miracle, I don't think it would convince me.

James: That's because you've closed your mind about miracles. My best friend told me about one that happened in her family, and I took her word for it.

Kevin: I bet there was a natural explanation for it if she had only known.

The geography teacher who took Helen for religious education did not believe in miracles. He gave four reasons for his disbelief, of which two appealed to science and two appealed to the unreliability of human testimony. The first two were:

1 that science shows miracles to be impossible,
2 that supposed 'miracles' can all be explained scientifically – as Kevin thought.

There has already been some discussion about **1** in the previous chapter, and about **2** in chapter 3, where it was pointed out that 'explaining' is not the same as 'explaining away'. In the account of the crossing of the Red Sea, for example, the *physical means* of the event *is* explained '... the LORD drove the sea back with a strong east wind...' (Exodus 14:21). There is, of course, no suggestion that this explains it away! The crossing of the Red Sea is an exception, however, for the Bible does not usually explain the mechanisms of miracles. That does not necessarily mean that they have no explanations. Neither does it mean that, if we had explanations, the miracles would have been 'explained away'.

> The wonder of a miracle is not that God is great enough to mess about with Nature, but that God is great enough to be 'mindful of man' ... A miracle declares His concern, not because He has acted where He does not normally act, but because His action has differed from what He is normally expected to do.
> (R L F Boyd *Faith in this Space Age*, 1963)

One reason for the Bible's lack of explanation of miracles might be the need to avoid distraction from the central concern, which is the *meaning* of miracles, not how they are accomplished. In the story of the burning bush (Exodus 3:1–6), for example,

> With the typical scientific attitude Moses said when he saw that phenomenon, 'I will go over and see this strange sight – why the bush does not burn up.' That is the typical scientific attitude. He was about to advance and investigate when the voice came, saying, 'Do not come any closer. Take off your sandals, for the place where you are standing is holy ground'. You do not investigate here, you worship, in reverence and in awe. (D Martyn Lloyd-Jones *The Approach to Truth: Scientific and Religious*, 1963, p 22, Tyndale Press)

A preoccupation with microscopes and meters, in order

to discover the mechanisms of a miracle, may result in our missing the purpose of it, which is to reveal the glory of God.

The other reasons that Helen's geography teacher gave for rejecting miracles were:

3 that people who believe in miracles probably imagine everything,
4 that such people are gullible in believing what they want to believe. (This reason is, of course, a double-edged sword which may wound the sceptic as much as the sceptic imagines it will wound the believer.)

Hume's view of miracles

There is nothing novel about the geography teacher's four reasons for dismissing miracles. They have been used over and over again, both before and since. The first two, as I mentioned earlier, appeal to science and the second two question the reliability of human testimony – as did Samantha at the beginning of the chapter. Similar reasons were stated very succinctly in a short chapter in *An Enquiry concerning Human Understanding* by the eighteenth-century philosopher, David Hume. Although Hume was not the only one to make the points, these few pages deeply affected people's thinking both at the time and since. They are worth looking at because since then most of the arguments against miracles have been based on them. Hume began by saying:

I flatter myself, that I have discovered an argument . . . which, if just, will, with the wise and learned, be an everlasting check to all kinds of superstitious delusion, and consequently, will be useful as long as the world endures. For so long, I presume, will the accounts of miracles and prodigies be found in all history, sacred and profane.

The chapter, *Of Miracles*, falls into two parts. Part one argues against miracles on the basis of a view of science that Hume assumed in advance. Such a way of arguing is often described as being based on *a priori* reasoning. The term *a priori* literally means 'from the former', and indicates that the reasoning is based on principles *assumed* in advance.

Part two concerns the reliability of the testimonies offered in support of miracles, and concludes that such testimonies are always too weak. Since a testimony is a report made after the event, Part two may be said to be based on *a posteriori* reasoning. This term means 'from the latter' and is used to describe an argument, such as for the proposition 'miracles cannot happen', which is supported by appealing to observations.

Hume was concerned at any attempt to base Christianity's claims to truth upon miraculous events. He wrote of the difficulty of showing from history that miracles have occurred, and hence of the inadequacy of using miracles to show the truth of any religion.

He allowed that belief in miracles may be a matter of faith, but regarded miracles themselves as being contrary to reason. Such a view, however, encourages the common but unjustified idea that faith and reason are separate from each other. Faith, in a biblical context, is always seen as based on facts, otherwise it is credulity. It involves actions based on evidence external to the individual.

In response to Hume, it needs to be made clear that the Bible does not base its claims to truth on the verifiability of miracles. Miracles are presented as an integral part of its message, of the ministry of Jesus and that of the early church but, as was indicated in chapter 4, they are not claimed as knock-down proofs. For the Bible records, as already noted, that some miracles draw their power from a source other than God.

Hume's 'Uniformity of Nature' argument

Hume expressed his argument against miracles, based on the Uniformity of Nature, as follows:

> A miracle is a violation of the laws of nature; and as a firm and unalterable experience has established these laws, the proof against a miracle, from the very nature of the fact, is as entire as any argument from experience can possibly be imagined.

In order to judge the strength of this argument, the phrase 'a firm and unalterable experience has established these laws', needs to be looked at rather carefully.

'Firm and unalterable experience' could mean that when the natural world is carefully observed, no exceptions are seen to the regular patterns of events. Those who claim to have seen miracles would naturally deny this. But for most of the earth's history, nobody has been making observations. So how can anyone be confident that 'unalterable experience has established these laws'? Only by assuming that things were carrying on in exactly the same way when they were not being observed as when they were. But that is to *assume* the Uniformity of Nature and the absence of miracles, which is the very thing that Hume was setting out to *prove*! Attempts to show that miracles cannot happen, *because* of the Uniformity of Nature, involve a circular argument.

For all except those people who are sure they have witnessed a miracle, the case for miracles rests upon the reliability of the testimonies of other people who claim to have seen them. If those people are dead, then it depends upon the reliability of the reports of those people's testimonies.

The testamentary evidence for miracles is a matter quite separate from the scientific issues with which this book is mainly concerned. But it merits some remarks since Hume's other main thrust against miracles was an attempt to discredit the testimony of those who claimed to have witnessed them.

Hume's 'unreliability of human testimony' argument

Hume expressed the view that:

> It is no miracle that a man, seemingly in good health, should die on a sudden . . . But it is a miracle, that a dead man should come to life; because that has never been observed in any age or country. There must, therefore, be a uniform experience against every miraculous event, otherwise the event would not merit that appellation. And as uniform experience amounts to a proof, there is here a direct and full *proof*, from the nature of the fact, against the existence of any miracle.

The form of this argument is:

● that there *must* be 'uniform experience' against miracles or else they would not be called miracles, and then
● that if 'uniform experience amounts to a proof', miracles cannot happen.

There are at least two criticisms that may be made. First, if something would only be called a miracle if there was uniform experience against it, then, on that definition, a miracle is something which cannot happen. This is a matter of logic, not experience. It is only so because of the way 'miracle' has been defined. It is Hume's *assumption* that experience is uniform that is open to question.

Second, Hume asserts in support of his case that a dead man coming to life 'has never been observed in any age or country'. He dismisses, without consideration, the Christian claims that just such an event *has* occurred, and more than once. Jesus is reported in the Gospels as having raised three people from the dead, eventually to die again. Furthermore, and this is foundational to Christianity, Jesus is himself said to have risen from the dead to live for ever.

Hume discounts such reports of human testimony as mistaken, or as lies. He argues in four ways against human testimony as a reliable means of establishing miracles.

All the witnesses are inadequate
First, he asserts the inadequacy of all witnesses, saying:

> . . . there is not to be found, in all history, any miracles attested by a sufficient number of men, of such unquestioned good-sense, education, and learning, as to secure us against all delusion in themselves.

But Hume is not always consistent. For, in discussing certain miracles reported in France 'upon the tomb of Abbé Paris', he acknowledges that:

> . . . many of the miracles were immediately proved upon the spot, before judges of unquestioned integrity, attested by witnesses of credit and distinction, in a learned age.

So how does he try to get himself out of his own dilemma? Answering his own question, he says:

> . . . what have we to oppose to such a cloud of witnesses, but the absolute impossibility or miraculous nature of the events, which they relate? And this surely, in the eyes of all reasonable people, will alone be regarded as a sufficient refutation.

In other words, although Hume claims to be looking dispassionately at the matter of evidence, he has in fact already made up his mind in advance that *no* amount of evidence will convince him that a miracle could take place.

Human testimony is unreliable

Second, he asserts the unreliability of human testimony, dismissing all reports of miracles as untrustworthy because people love to exaggerate and gossip:

> The passion of *surprise* and *wonder*, arising from miracles, being an agreeable emotion, gives a sensible tendency towards the belief of those events . . . even those who cannot enjoy this pleasure immediately, nor can believe those miraculous events . . . love to partake of the satisfaction at second-hand or by rebound, and place a pride and delight in exciting the admiration of others.

But the fact that people *do* like talking about unusual events does not of itself mean that the events did not happen. Our tabloid newspapers daily indulge in exaggeration and gossip, but that does not mean that there are never any events corresponding to these reports that pander to a love of the spectacular.

People who see 'miracles' are gullible

Third, Hume says that reports of miracles 'are observed chiefly to abound among ignorant and barbarous nations'. This may be an aside directed at the people of biblical times, as opposed to those of the supposedly enlightened, Western, eighteenth century. But it is arrogant to dismiss people of other times and other cultures as stupid when compared with Western moderns. On such a criterion, Hume's own generation would have to fall before a 'superior' twentieth century! His criticism fails to distinguish between the reporting of an unusual event and the interpretation which might be placed on that event. The former is a matter of personal integrity, of which neither the eighteenth century nor the twentieth century has a monopoly.

The rival claims of different religions cancel each other out

Fourth, Hume claims that different religions have their own miracle stories, which are used to establish the claims of the religion concerned over against those of rival religions.

> Every miracle, therefore, pretended to have been wrought in any of these religions . . . is to establish the particular system to which it is attributed; so it has the same force, though more indirectly, to overthrow every other system. In destroying a rival system, it likewise destroys the credit of those miracles, on which that system was established.

In short, Hume sees the rival claims of different religions as cancelling each other out. But, in view of the earlier points, that miracles are not presented as knock-down proofs of the truth of Christianity, and also that the Bible records miracles that are not attributed to God, any apparent cutting edge to Hume's fourth argument disappears.

Assessing 'Of Miracles'

A reading of *Of Miracles* shows more than once that no amount of testamentary evidence will convince Hume that miracles have occurred. It is also clear that if the weight of testimony seems to be becoming too heavy for comfort, he shifts his ground by retreating from the 'testimony' argument to the 'laws of nature' argument. 'Hume has in effect set up an invincible naturalism.' This kind of *a priori* reasoning has something in common with that of Helen's father, for whom even the fact of his daughter's return to health was not sufficient evidence that miracles could happen today.

It seems that Hume is prepared to trust human testimony if it provides 'uniform experience against every miraculous event', but distrusts it when it counts against his case. This is inconsistent, and open to the charge of special pleading.

Hume holds 'a suspicion concerning any matter of fact' when the witnesses 'are but few'. But it is not simply the number of witnesses that matters: their reliability, or otherwise, is at least as relevant. For example, when some fishermen netted a Coelacanth in 1938, it falsified a scientific theory that these creatures had been extinct for 60 million years. But suppose, instead, that an expert in marine biology had caught it, identified it and lost it while trying to get it on board. Until another one was caught, the world would have been entirely dependent on this one person's account of the unlikely event. The basis for weighing the testimony could only have been the reliability of the witness.

It is perfectly proper to ask whether an unlikely event has any precedent. If it has, it makes it more credible. But ultimately the issue concerns the way in which we assess evidence. Certainly, the evidence for something that has such far-reaching consequences as the resurrection has, needs to be examined thoroughly, as will be shown in chapter 10. But claims about even such an unlikely event as the resurrection should not be ruled out *a priori*, without examining the evidence. If the unusual is ruled out simply on the grounds of lack of precedent, then anything new will automatically be excluded, even if true!

Quite apart from miracles, many events are seen by only a few. But the testimony of the lone astronomer who happens to be the sole witness of a supernova is in no way refuted by the scores of people who were not looking at the time and who could testify that they saw no such thing.

8

Where does God come in?

Jason: I think we should 'soft-pedal' all this talk of miracles if we want people to believe in Christianity in a scientific age.

Sally: I agree! Surely Christianity stands a better chance of success without talk of virgins having babies and people rising from the dead!

Amanda: But surely, the issue is not, 'are such things easy to believe?' but 'did they happen?'

Peter: Does it matter whether they did, or not? Isn't it the teaching that matters?

Susan: Yes, of course the teaching matters, but so do miracles like the virgin birth – they're an integral part of the teaching. If God comes into the world to make himself known personally, maybe he needs to come in in a different way from the rest of us.

Susan, like Helen, talks about God being known personally. When Helen described her miraculous cure she did not talk about God as a 'concept'. She did not use philosophical language and refer to God as 'transcendent, conscious agency', although that might have been appropriate at a different level of discussion. She said things like, 'I was alone to pray and ask God for guidance.' Also, she believed that God was speaking to her. In the first instance, she said that this was through the speaker: 'I knew ... that the Lord had surely spoken to Tom about me.' Later, she spoke of an inward conviction: 'I felt Him tell me to stand up.'

Helen was putting into words a deep conviction that she had encountered God, that he had in some way come into her life. This thoroughly orthodox belief, she would have explained, was the fulfilment of Jesus' promise that, after rising from the dead, he would send the Holy Spirit, and that in this way the Father and the Son would enter people's lives.

Helen might also have explained, if pressed further, that all this was conditional on Jesus' return to his Father, which in turn depended upon his having come from the Father in the first place. So *incarnation*, like *resurrection* is a key miracle in the Christian story. The resurrection is the subject of chapter 10; in this chapter and the next we shall think about the incarnation and the virgin birth.

Incarnation and virgin birth

'Incarnation' means 'embodied in flesh', and it is the word commonly used in the Christian claim that God entered his created spacetime, in order to speak directly to us. John expresses this majestically at the beginning of his Gospel. Since speaking involves words, he refers to Jesus Christ as the 'Word':

> In the beginning was the Word, and the Word was with God, and the Word was God. He was with God in the beginning ... The Word became flesh and lived for a while among us. We have seen his glory, the glory of the one and only Son who came from the

Father, full of grace and truth. (John 1:1-3, 14)

Matthew's Gospel gives a different perspective on the incarnation, saying that the conception of Jesus was not by the normal union of man and woman but by a miraculous act within Mary's body — 'what is conceived in her is from the Holy Spirit' (Matthew 1:20).

There is little more to be said about this than has already been said about miracles in general. Some people have commented that the rare biological event of *parthenogenesis* (reproduction by means of an ovum capable of development without male fertilisation) will only produce a *female* offspring. But this misses the point. The claim about the virgin birth of Jesus is not that a natural, if rare, biological event has occurred, but that something unique has taken place. Science, which describes the normal, cannot say whether or not it could have occurred.

Authenticity?

Evidence for the virgin birth of Jesus would have to be historical, and the only person in a position to be quite certain that his mother had not had sexual relations with a man, would be Mary herself. So the possibility of confirmation is zero, by the nature of the case. We must therefore pursue a different line of enquiry if we are to explore whether this unique claim is part of the authentic story. One test for authenticity is to see whether such an event fits in coherently with the character of Jesus and with other known aspects of his life on earth.

Dorothy Sayers, the author, introduces this test procedure by considering the difference between good and bad art forms in writing. C S Lewis develops her idea:

If you are writing a story, miracles or abnormal events may be bad art, or they may not. If, for example, you are writing an ordinary realistic novel and have got your characters into a hopeless muddle, it would be quite intolerable if you suddenly cut the knot and secured a happy ending by having a fortune left to the hero from an unexpected quarter. On the other hand there is nothing against taking as your subject from the outset the adventures of a man who inherits an unexpected fortune. The unusual event is perfectly permissible if it is what you are really writing *about*; it is an artistic crime if you simply drag it in by the heels to get yourself out of a hole. (C S Lewis *Miracles*, 1947, p 118, Geoffrey Bles)

The incarnation *is* the story. It is 'The Grand Miracle' towards which everything leads and from which everything develops. So,

Since the Incarnation, if it is a fact, holds this central position, and since we are assuming that we do not know it to have happened on historical grounds, we are in a position which may be illustrated by the following analogy. Let us suppose we possess parts of a novel or a symphony. Someone now brings us a newly discovered piece of manuscript and says, 'This is the missing part of the work. This is the chapter on which the whole plot of the novel really turned. This is the main theme of the symphony.' Our business would be to see whether the new passage, if admitted to the central place which the discoverer claimed for it, did actually illuminate all the parts we had already seen and 'pull them together'. (C S Lewis, *op cit*, p 132)

Similar tests of coherence may be applied to the virgin birth as the means of incarnation. But we shall not discuss here the theological aspect of the virgin birth as the way in which Jesus Christ became truly human, yet without sin. That has been explored in many theological texts. Our immediate concern is with the virgin birth as a miracle.

Myth: a slippery word?

Some years ago, *The Myth of God Incarnate* was published. A reviewer asked, 'Why are they so attracted to the word [myth]?' and answered the rhetorical question, 'Partly, it seems, because it is provocative. Yet it is a spurious provocativeness, derived solely from the overtones of something delusive and false.' (*The Expository Times* (1977) **85** [4])

'Myth' has been called a 'slippery word' because it means different things to different theologians, depending upon which particular sense is favoured. The situation is made worse by individual writers using the word in several different ways. But to the non-specialist, 'myth' usually implies a legend, something which is not true.

The reviewer mentioned above pointed out that the contributors 'use the word [myth] over 200 times . . . yet few attempts are made to define the sense in which the word is used'. But however unclearly the word 'myth' may have been used in that collection of essays, one thing seemed clear from the preface: the book was intended as a response to the view that 'the pressure upon Christianity is as strong as ever to go on adapting itself into something which can be believed – believed by honest and thoughtful people'. This, however, seems to place an enormous emphasis on people's ability to believe. And if 'something which can be believed' is to be the criterion for what should be taught as Christianity, how would it appear in the light of the following conversation?

'I can't believe *that*!' said Alice.

'Can't you?' the Queen said in a pitying tone. 'Try again: draw a long breath, and shut your eyes.'

Alice laughed. 'There's no use trying,' she said: 'one *can't* believe impossible things.'

'I daresay you haven't had much practice,' said the Queen. 'When I was your age, I always did it for half-an-hour a day. Why, sometimes I've believed as many as six impossible things before breakfast.'

If the ability of people to believe is the key factor, why not get everyone to practise believing, like the Red Queen? Clearly that is silly. What is important is not our ability to believe, but whether what we believe is true or not. If it is true, then we have to reckon with it, whether we find it difficult to believe or not. A modern example from science illustrates the point. Suppose someone asked if it would be possible to cut a photographic transparency in pieces, shine a light through one of the pieces and then see the whole picture. Most people, unless they were familiar with holograms and lasers, would emphatically reply, 'no!' But, unlikely though it sounds, it can be done. Some of the detail is sacrificed, but the whole picture can be seen.

When this first became known it seemed incredible, unless you happened to understand the physics. Nowadays, the phenomenon is more widely known so the usefulness of the example is diminishing. But we can still see the point that the truth or otherwise of the account is the key issue, not whether or not the account is believable. What we find believable is very dependent upon our 'common sense' – upon what our previous experience has led us to expect.

The policy of admitting only what is currently believable is no new phenomenon. Some years ago, after Bishop Robinson had written his much-publicised *Honest to God*, he published another book called, *But That I Can't Believe!* In it he applauded naturalistic interpretations of miracles, which made no calls upon 'modern man' to believe anything that, with his present understanding of the world, he could not grasp. He quoted with approval his daughter's interpretation of the account in Matthew 8 of Jesus healing Peter's mother-in-law:

I know why Peter's mother-in-law took to her bed. I think she was just fed up with Peter spending all his time going around with Jesus instead of looking after her daughter. *But when Jesus came to her house and she saw the sort of person he was, she wanted to get up and do things for people.* (J A T Robinson *But That I Can't Believe!* 1967, p 31, Fontana)

The story of the feeding of the five thousand has sometimes been emptied of any miraculous element by people claiming that the little boy's unselfish action, in sharing his packed lunch, prompted others to do the same. But does this make the story easier to believe, or does it trivialise it? Bishop Robinson thought some such explanation made it more believable, and recounted the story of five students on a trek, during which they had begged for everything in order to identify with the world's starving millions. As they distributed the things they had received, they saw the event as a 'miracle of sharing'. So John Robinson's verdict on the New Testament account was that

> that story is not the physical miracle of a multiplication of loaves but the spiritual miracle that can be sparked off when even one person is inspired to share.
> (Robinson, *op cit*, p 32)

He has retained the word 'miracle' in the second part of the sentence, but has in fact shifted its meaning, so that no one, reading this story, will be called upon to believe anything outside of their own middle-sized existence. It is not that any clearer understanding of the biblical text has been provided. His prime criterion for interpretation appears to be, 'Can I believe it?' But is that criterion adequate? Even at the mundane level of science, our knowledge is clearly partial. New wonders are being discovered daily. 'Knowledge is proud that he has learn'd so much; Wisdom is humble that he knows no more', said Cowper. How much more likely that the knowledge of God will be full of surprises!

Priority and importance

In the Appendix, I refer to Bishop David Jenkins' comment that, 'The Resurrection narratives are far more about encounters and namings and joyful recognitions than about the empty tomb.' He parallels this statement with one about the virgin birth, saying, 'The Birth narratives are far more about the obedience of Mary and Joseph in response to the unique graciousness of God than about Mary's physical virginity.' (D E Jenkins *God, Miracle and the Church of England*, 1987, p 6, SCM Press)

Now, those statements of priority may well be true. I am not concerned to debate them here, because they are irrelevant to the immediate task of exposing a bad argument. For it certainly does not follow that, because one thing is more important than another, the other is not important as well. To use such statements to divert attention from the importance of the virgin birth and the bodily resurrection of Christ is to use, however unintentionally, a debating trick – distraction.

I have no wish to be credulous, but if Jesus was whom he claimed to be, what problem does the virgin birth present? May not God, the ultimate giver of every sperm-initiated baby, do things differently if he so wishes? If the virgin birth seems difficult to believe, it may be that, in the words of J B Phillips' book title, 'Your God is too small'!

Those who already accept that God can work in unusual ways in his creation are unlikely to find more difficulties over the miracle of a virgin birth than over any other. But those who have already decided, with Matthew Arnold, that 'miracles do not happen' will not be disposed to accept this one either.

But the idea of incarnation, of the Creator stepping into the creation, is an intriguing one, which we shall develop in the next chapter, from a literary comparison suggested by Dorothy Sayers.

9

Meet the Author

Stephen: I think of God as being like a clockmaker.

Frances: Well, I see him more as some kind of a force.

Sandra: I think the Bible's picture of him as a father takes a lot of beating. How do you think of God, Dorothy?

Dorothy: 'As a living author.'

The 'conversations' which head the chapters are typical, but fictitious. Dorothy's comment, however, is a genuine quotation from Dorothy Sayers. She compared God to the author of a book in which we are all characters. The comparison begs the question, of course, as to whether the biblical picture of God's relationship with us *is* comparable to that of an author with the characters in a book – or the actors in a play, to use a similar analogy. If the comparison *does* hold good, you could say that when Helen, as she claimed, met God as her Lord earlier in her life, it was like meeting the 'Author'.

Comparisons are usually interesting and creative

because they can expand our understanding in surprising ways. Initially, however, we are unsure about how far they can be pressed, and there are pitfalls in using them. But it is worth taking the trouble to avoid their pitfalls in order to benefit from their usefulness.

One deficiency of the analogy is the inadequate account it appears to take of human freedom and accountability. The author of a play writes the lines and the actors speak them. Although the player may *ad lib* a little, the script is fixed, and the author has determined the outcome of the play by the time the players are on stage. True, there have been plays in which a number of alternative endings are scripted, and the one to be enacted on the night is decided by the throw of a coin during the play – but this is unusual.

There is one sense, however, in which this rather deterministic model does appear to mirror biblical teaching. For, despite human choices and people's attempts to thwart God's purposes, in the end his plan will be accomplished. Such was the case with Christ's crucifixion. The human-freedom aspect of his death is highlighted by Peter's accusation, on the day of Pentecost, that 'you, with the help of wicked men, put him to death by nailing him to the cross'. God held them accountable and, through Peter, called them to repent. But it is still the Author's 'play', for 'This man was handed over to you by God's set purpose and foreknowledge' (Acts 2:23). It will still be the Author's 'play', also, when God fulfils 'his good pleasure, which he purposed in Christ, to be put into effect when the times will have reached their fulfilment – to bring all things in heaven and on earth together under one head, even Christ' (Ephesians 1:9–10).

Authors reveal their minds in their books; they say what they are thinking. So Dorothy Sayers entitled her book, in which she compares God to an author, *The Mind of the Maker*. In the past, the physical world and the Bible have often been thought of as 'God's Two Books' in which he reveals his mind. The physical world has been seen as the

Book of Nature – the 'Book of God's Works', and the Bible as the Book of Scripture – the 'Book of God's Words', God being the 'Author' of both.

Sometimes, Dorothy Sayers continues, authors write a number of books, which may include an autobiography – a book by the author, about the author.

> Christian doctrine further affirms that the Mind of the Maker was also incarnate personally and uniquely. Examining our analogy for something to which this may correspond, we may say that God wrote His own autobiography ...
>
> ... It is unique, because the author appears, personally and without disguise, as a character in his own story. (D Sayers *The Mind of the Maker*, 1942, pp 70f, Methuen)

In this way she compares the incarnation of Jesus Christ to the writing of a story in which the author actually appears within the story as one of the characters – a literary device which has been used a number of times by different writers.

One Christmas, for a Family Service, I tried to create something that would convey a sense of the incongruity of the incarnation, of the author becoming an actor in his own play. The result was the following story: its lack of literary merit requires an apology in advance – not least to the late Enid Blyton!

Noddy's surprise visitor

It was a cold winter's afternoon just before Christmas and Noddy had spent two hours doing his Christmas shopping. He had bought a lovely present for Bert Monkey. Noddy pulled up outside Bert's front door and stopped right on the double yellow line. He hoped Mr Plod, the policeman, wouldn't come by, but, just in case, he switched on his hazard lights to pretend he had broken down. Wasn't Noddy naughty?

He walked quickly up the garden path, his wobbly hat going nod, nod, nod, and he knocked at the front door. When Bert Monkey came to the door his face lit up with pleasure – even more so when he saw the large parcel Noddy was carrying. 'Come in, Noddy,' said Bert, 'I was just going to have tea. Do join me.'

They had just sat down to a tea of crumpets, jam and cream cakes when the front door bell went ring! ring! ring!

'Mr Plod!' thought Noddy guiltily. 'He's come to book me for parking on the double yellow line!' Bert went to the door and Noddy heard a lady's voice. Presently Bert returned, looking very puzzled. 'Who is it?' said Noddy.

'She says her name's Enid; and she wants to come in,' replied Bert Monkey.

'Enid who?' asked Noddy.

'I don't know,' said Bert, 'but I'd better let her in – it's freezing with the front door open.'

A middle-aged lady came in and smiled at them both. 'Hello!' she said. 'My name is Enid Blyton, but don't bother to tell me your names. I know who *you* are.'

Noddy and Bert were too puzzled to say anything and the lady went on. 'I can see you're looking puzzled. What I mean is, I know you because I made you – you might even say I *created* you.'

'What do you mean?' said Noddy crossly. 'Don't play jokes! I'm tired! I've just spent two hours Christmas shopping!'

'I'm not joking,' said the lady. 'I know it's difficult for you to understand, but without me, you wouldn't be here to do any Christmas shopping – and your shopping only took five seconds in my time. I mustn't stop, though. I've got my own Christmas shopping to do. But I did want to drop in and wish you both a Happy Christmas!'

After the lady had gone, Bert Monkey and Noddy sat and looked at each other for a long time before either of them said a word. Noddy was the first to break the silence with a single word. 'Crackers!' he said.

I had warned the children that it was a badly written story, but I had also asked them to put up their hands when they felt it became *really* odd. Of course the hands started to go up when Enid Blyton came in.

The disturbing claims of Jesus

One of the points of my story was to show how odd it must have seemed when a local man came and made the claims that Jesus made to his contemporaries. 'Your father Abraham rejoiced at the thought of seeing my day; he saw it and was glad,' said Jesus. The puzzled Jews replied, 'You are not yet fifty years old ... and you have seen Abraham!' (John 8:56f). We tend to overlook the sheer incongruity of the claim that the son of the local carpenter should be the Author of the whole show, including his hearers.

My story made another point, for which I claim no originality, that 'author-time' differs from 'actor-time'. It took only five seconds of Enid Blyton's time to give Noddy a two-hour Christmas-shopping trip; the time-scale of her story was her own creation, and it had no being apart from her. In this world's story our time is itself part of the created order. As Saint Augustine put it, creation is *with* time, not *in* time – a picture echoed by modern cosmology. But whatever does it mean to talk about God's time, by analogy with ours? And yet the literary device of a story may help us, nevertheless, to expand our thinking, to conceive that in God's domain (another metaphor) things might function differently from the way they do in our own.

> With the Lord a day is like a thousand years, and a
> thousand years are like a day. (2 Peter 3:8)

The disturbing sensation, caused by this mixing of dimensions and time-scales, reminds me of the feelings I had as a child when I looked at the picture on my toy carpet-sweeper. The picture was that of a child pushing a similar toy carpet-sweeper. And on the carpet-sweeper in the picture was a small picture of a child pushing a carpet-sweeper! And on the carpet sweeper in the small picture, you could just see it, was the tiniest of pictures of you-know-what! You may have had a similar sense on looking at a model village which includes a model of the model village which includes . . .

So when Jesus said, 'I came from the Father and entered the world; now I am leaving the world and going back to the Father' (John 16:28) it is not surprising that his hearers felt a sense of unreality and incongruity. It may have been a little bit like the feeling one has if, after avidly following the adventures of a hero in a series of books, one suddenly meets the author!

Encountering the Author?

> The itch for personally knowing authors torments most of us; we feel that if we could somehow get at the man himself, we should obtain more help and satisfaction from him than from his chosen self-revelation . . . it is desirable to bear in mind – when dealing with the human maker at any rate – that his chosen way of revelation *is* through his works. To persist in asking, as many of us do, 'What did you mean by this book?' is to invite bafflement: the book itself is what the writer means. (D Sayers, *op cit*, p 45)

These words of Dorothy Sayers give food for thought, because they describe a common experience. Many people feel that if only they could, physically, enter into dialogue with God, they would understand much more than by simply reading the Bible. But the Book is the 'Mind of the Maker' and, in reading it, the Author is encountered.

The comparison with a human author is even better when we come to a particular type of book, an autobiography. I once met ex-President Nixon's 'hatchet man', Charles Colson. He had been implicated in the Watergate scandal and had been sent to prison for it. Through the ordeal he had been converted to Christianity and had written his autobiography, *Born Again*. So, then, was this man the humbled and changed person the autobiography gave one to believe he would be? Did the man match the book? My firm impression was that he did.

The sense of 'meeting the author' is a reasonable illustration of what can best be described as the 'experience of encounter', to which Helen referred, when someone becomes a Christian. One experiences a deep, inner conviction of knowing God and of being known by him. This inner witness is described by Paul in the words, 'the Spirit himself testifies with our spirit that we are God's children' (Romans 8:16).

The autobiography comparison may be appropriately concluded with some more of Dorothy Sayers' thought-provoking words:

> [Autobiography] is an infallible self-betrayal. The truth about the writer's personality will out, in spite of itself; any illusions which he may entertain about himself become fearfully apparent the moment he begins to handle himself as a created character ... If, however, the author either consciously or unconsciously tries to incarnate himself as something other than what he is, there will be a falseness in the artistic expression ... the truth of what he says about himself is tested by the truth of the form in which he says it ...

For this reason, no considerations of false reverence

should prevent us from subjecting the incarnations of creators to the severest tests of examination. It is right that they should be pulled about and subjected to the most searching kind of enquiry. If the structure is truly knit, it will stand any strain, and prove its truth by its toughness. Pious worshippers, whether of mortal or immortal artists, do their deities little honour by treating their incarnations as something too sacred for rough handling; they only succeed in betraying a fear lest the structure should prove flimsy or false. But the writing of autobiography is a dangerous business; it is a mark or either great insensitiveness to danger or of an almost supernatural courage. Nobody but a god can pass unscathed through the searching ordeal of incarnation. (D Sayers, *op cit*, pp 73f)

10

Back from the dead?

Alex: All this stuff about Jesus rising from the dead sounds like wishful thinking to me. Anyway, how could you ever know whether something like that happened so long ago?

Deborah: Just because something is supposed to have happened long ago doesn't rule it out – otherwise every historian would be out of a job!

Harry: I don't think Jesus could have been dead when he was placed in the tomb. Medical science shows dead people don't come back to life. Does it matter anyway?

Sandra: Yes it does! The resurrection – like the incarnation – is an integral part of the Christian message. If God *hasn't* appeared in the world we are left with a story of a good man, another religious leader. If Christ didn't rise from the dead, after he'd died for our sins, how do we know he has power over death? And if he *is* still dead, what hope is there for help today?

Liz: I think Deborah has a point when she says

historians would be out of a job. But they're not. They still carry on their profession. I suppose ancient events leave their mark on society, and there are the written records too. So maybe it's like a detective story – you just have to piece the bits of evidence together.

All the general points that have already been made about miracles apply to the claim that Jesus Christ rose from the dead, a miracle to which we must pay special attention, as we did to the incarnation. For it is foundational to Christianity, being God's vindication of Christ's death for our sins. The early Christians were in no doubt about its importance, and the apostle Paul sums up any discussion about it with these succinct words:

> . . . if Christ has not been raised, your faith is futile; you are still in your sins. Then those also who have fallen asleep in Christ are lost. If only for this life we have hope in Christ, we are to be pitied more than all men. (1 Corinthians 15:17–19)

The main reason for considering the resurrection here is that it raises important points about the methods of assessing evidence for miracles; for the issue is an historical one (did Christ rise from the dead?) not a scientific one (do people normally rise from the dead?). Therefore historical evidence, rather than scientific data, plays the major part in judging it to be true or false. The evidence available to us today for the resurrection of Jesus Christ is both *indirect* and *cumulative*, and it also includes the *direct* evidence of personal encounter. (Chapter 11 will deal with the handling of different kinds of evidence.) Debate about the resurrection also makes us recognise how carefully we need to scrutinise *any* claim that a miracle has taken place, for the implications of such a claim may be very far-reaching. This is certainly so in the case of the resurrection. Does believing in its truth make one guilty of credulity, or is there sufficient evidence for one to claim that it is a well-grounded belief?

Science, for reasons given earlier, cannot say, before the event, whether the resurrection of the body could occur. Its role, in this type of enquiry, is limited. It may be a source of helpful analogies; the resurrection of the body might be compared with the re-embodying of a computer programme in a new computer after the original computer has been destroyed. But an analogy does not prove anything. It can only *illustrate* something for which there must be independent evidence. Science may also assist in historical research. For instance, radioactive dating has been used in investigating the authenticity of the Turin Shroud.

A matter of history

Claims about whether or not Jesus Christ rose from the dead are historical ones, to be judged by the canons of historical enquiry. Professor Ives summarises the task facing him as an historian:

> Collecting data is the first stage of the historical process. The second is assessing it. This is a matter of assigning relative weight to individual items and exploring possible relationships and disconnections, probing – because this is history and not natural science – motives as well as action. Proposing a general conclusion or hypothesis is the final stage, a considered verdict by the historian. In a single enquiry he has moved from detective to counsel and has ended up as a jury of one. (E W Ives *God in History*, 1979, p 28, Lion Publishing)

In many historical enquiries, the historian may remain fairly detached from the study. It is different with the resurrection of Jesus Christ. J N D Anderson, formerly Professor of Oriental Law in the University of London, wrote a booklet entitled, *The Evidence for the Resurrection* which opens with these words:

> Easter is not primarily a comfort, but a challenge . . .
> If it is true, then it is the supreme fact of history; and
> to fail to adjust one's life to its implications means
> irreparable loss. But if it is not true, if Christ be not
> risen, then the whole of Christianity is a fraud, foisted
> on the world by a company of consummate liars, or,
> at best, deluded simpletons.

Professor Anderson then spreads out some of the evidence that gives us good grounds for confidence about the resurrection, confidence that this event, though unprecedented and so long ago, did actually happen. The following paragraphs give some of his main points.

Reviewing the evidence

The documentary evidence is good. The events are much better attested than are extra-biblical ones of comparable antiquity. It has been said that the Bible should be treated like any other book for the purposes of historical enquiry. That is unexceptionable, but sometimes it is treated like *no* other book and wholesale doubts are cast on the integrity of its writers in a way that would never be countenanced in a consideration of secular writers.

The documentary evidence rests primarily on the written testimonies of six witnesses, Matthew, Mark, Luke, John, Peter and Paul. Their accounts were written reasonably close in time to the events they describe.

It has been claimed that the accounts of the resurrection are deliberate inventions, but such a claim would not be easy to sustain. To deceive in this way would be completely out of character for those who gave the world the highest moral and ethical teaching it has ever known. Also, living a known lie does not have the effect of turning cowards into bold people; yet the disciples who deserted Christ at the time of his arrest later became a force that

Imperial Rome had to reckon with! Many of the early Christians died gladly for their faith in their Lord, whom they believed to have risen from the dead. Others were tortured. And yet no whisper – uttered in disillusionment or extracted under great pain – has come down to us from antiquity of anyone 'spilling the beans', admitting that the resurrection was invented.

The idea that certain original events were embellished, and became legends, is another suggested alternative to a resurrection. This, too, runs into difficulties, for the accounts do not read like legends, and besides, the time between the supposed events and their earliest records is not long enough to permit the growth of legends.

Accounting for the empty tomb

The greatest stumbling block to the idea that Jesus never actually arose from the dead is, of course, the empty tomb. The apostles first preached in Jerusalem, within walking distance of the tomb; it was open to anyone to check whether or not it was occupied. But those who are unwilling to concede that the empty tomb suggests the resurrection of Jesus may find one of several alternative explanations to be more attractive:

(a) that the body had been stolen,
(b) that the disciples had mistaken the tomb, partly because of the dim light of early morning and partly because of their confused state of mind, and
(c) that Christ was not actually dead when he was laid in the tomb.

(a) If the body was indeed stolen, by whom was it taken? If it was the disciples, a proposal which David Jenkins describes as 'the alternative rational and plausible explanation', then, apart from having to get past the guard, they would have had to put the corpse where it could never be found. The disciples would have lived their lives

– and in many cases sacrificed them – for something they knew to be a lie.

If it was the authorities who took the body, why did they not produce the mouldering remains when they wanted to scotch the rumour, which was turning Jerusalem upside down, that Christ had risen from the dead?

If it was grave-robbers, they too had to get past the guards. What was their motive, since they left behind the only valuable things, the spices and the graveclothes? Furthermore, no trace of the body was ever found.

(b) If the disciples had mistaken the tomb, the full light of day would have convinced them, and others too, for the correct tomb was still sealed.

(c) But perhaps Christ never died. After all, the soldiers were surprised, when they went to take him down, that he was dead already. However, as Josephus, the first-century historian, records, few people who had been nailed to a cross, even if taken down shortly afterwards, survived the ordeal. In Jesus' case, a spear had been put in his side and he had been swathed from head to foot in grave clothes soaked with materials having anaesthetic properties. Also, he was exhausted before the crucifixion.

Despite these hindrances, according to the theory, Jesus extracted himself from the bands of cloth wound round him from head to toe, and rolled away a stone which three women felt unable to tackle. Then he managed to get past the guards and later walk on nail-pierced feet with two disciples to Emmaus, leaving them with the firm impression that he was *Christus Victor*, the Prince of Life. There are difficulties with this view. Quite apart from the physical inconsistencies involved, it would make Christ a party to gross deception, which would be completely at variance with everything else recorded about him.

Alternatively, it has been suggested that the resurrection 'appearances' were hallucinations. One problem with this idea is that many people of differing psychologies were involved. Hallucinations tend to be different for each individual, rather than, as reported in the gospels, the same for many people. They also tend to be experienced by people of a certain type, and to be repeated, with greater or lesser frequency, over a period of time, but all the reported 'sightings' of Jesus were confined to forty days, never to recur.

The resurrection's historical consequences

Major events leave their place in history. If the resurrection is denied, some explanation still has to be found for certain historical matters:

● The jealousy guarded Jewish Sabbath became, for many, the Christian 'Sunday', the first day of the week. Why was this if the resurrection and subsequent events of 'Whitsunday' never took place?

● A group of cowards, who scattered at the arrest of their leader, became a people who 'turned the world upside down'. What happened to initiate this change?

● The historian, Tacitus (c AD 56–120), records that the crucifixion of Jesus 'checked that pernicious superstition for a short time, but it broke out afresh'. Why was this?

● To what did the Christian church owe its inception?

There are, of course, possible explanations other than the resurrection for all these matters. *Ad hoc* explanations of the details can always be found. So how can one hope to arrive at a true understanding when there are many small pieces of evidence, each of which may have other possible explanations? Clearly, the assessment of evidence is of central importance, and it is to this matter that we now turn.

11

'. . . and may be used in evidence'

Trevor: I despair, sometimes, about ever being sure of anything.

Stacey: That's because you're looking for the kinds of proof you only find in some branches of maths. People don't live like that! They simply want to know if there's enough evidence for action.

Ruth: Yes, I'd never have got married if I'd demanded absolute proofs for everything, like you do!

Paul: But how do you cope when there are lots of pieces of evidence, and they can all be interpreted in different ways?

Cumulative evidence

One way forward, when trying to make sense of a variety of pieces of evidence, is to judge what is the most unifying explanation. Which explanation accounts most economically for all the data? To put it in other words, what is the *cumulative* effect of all these pieces of evidence?

When we are piecing together evidence for some event

that is difficult to examine, such as an event in the distant past, we may not judge any single piece of evidence to be totally convincing by itself. Nevertheless, many small pieces of evidence may fit together very impressively. Like pieces of a jigsaw puzzle, they may join together to make a convincing whole. Professor Sir Robert Boyd gives a personal view of how the steady pressure of mounting evidence may build up a convincing, cumulative case in science and, in this case, Christian faith.

> When I first started doing research in physics the theory of the force between particles in the atomic nucleus was high on the list of important topics, and I recall how each new discovery gave rise to a new theory; or to look at it in another way, the number of possible modifications in the theory was roughly equal to the number of known facts. That situation is one with which the scientist is familiar, and it is a warning that something is wrong, that understanding has not yet been reached. It is required of true understanding that it brings coherence, makes sense of the whole. As I consider the things about Jesus of Nazareth, for me, at any rate, there seems to be only one possible conclusion. It is the one to which Saul the persecutor came in a flash upon the Damascus road: 'God was in Christ reconciling the world to himself.' (R L F Boyd *Can God be Known?* 1967, p 16 [adapted], IVP)

The building of a cumulative case is similar to the solution of the mystery in a detective story. Many small items of information are known to the police and to the detective – such as Agatha Christie's 'Miss Marple'. Each fragment of evidence has many possible explanations. But there is one conclusion that 'makes sense of the whole' and *this* is usually revealed in the last chapter. Despite all the efforts of the plodding policemen, it is only Miss Marple who can show how the guilt of someone she suspected in the first chapter accounts for all the fragments of evidence at one stroke!

Cumulative evidence may draw upon many small fragments of *direct* evidence and also many tiny pieces of *indirect* evidence. The direct evidence of our senses has limitations, in areas of science as well as in matters of spiritual beliefs. So we often have to resort to evidence of another kind, indirect evidence.

Indirect evidence

Evidence for something that cannot be seen must be indirect evidence. We meet it in all kinds of ways: for example, we conclude that a high-flying aircraft has gone by recently from the indirect evidence of a vapour trail in the sky. Similar vapour trails, in cloud chambers, enable the scientist to infer the presence of invisible electrons. The use of cloud chambers may seem a rather roundabout way to find out about elementary particles, but when dealing with electrons, which are too small to see, some such method must be used.

As in science, so with matters of religion: reasoned conclusions may be reached in a rather roundabout way. Sometimes this is in the nature of the topic. It is satisfying when things are simple, but if they are not we just have to accept them as they are. Einstein once said, 'Everything should be made as simple as possible, but not simpler.' Over-simplify, and the end result may be simplistic.

Although the use of evidence to settle questions of religion bears some similarity to its use in science, there are significant differences. For example, the indirect evidence provided by cloud chambers is for invisible *physical* 'objects', such as electrons. But God, although he, too, is invisible, is not a physical object. Also, the kinds of evidence that apply in the realm of belief are different from those that are relevant in scientific enquiry. But, nonetheless, they make up a 'cumulative case' and to this we now turn.

Evidence supporting religious belief

Religious experience

Religious beliefs are among the most widespread and persistent features of human societies. This does not of itself mean they must be true. That would be the fallacy of arguing from numbers – an illegitimate ploy of advertisers. Four million MiniMaxi owners *can* be wrong! But it does mean that such beliefs should be considered seriously. Christian believers have existed in every age since New Testament times and have come from all nationalities; they may have any age, occupation, or level of intellectual ability. Their witness on other matters would be treated seriously in a court of law, and due weight should be given to their testimony on this important issue.

Some people deny religious experience for the reason that they do not themselves share it. This may be unwise – the worlds of colour and sound are not called into question because some people are colour-blind or tone-deaf.

Natural Theology

'Theology' is 'the study of God' – 'God-talk'. Natural Theology concerns what can be known about God by simply looking at the natural world and using reason. Some people have thought that Natural Theology made it possible to prove God's existence by what are known as the traditional arguments for the existence of God. These include arguments based on the idea of God being the First Cause, on what appears to be design in the world, on our sense of right and wrong, and on the fact that there is a world at all.

Many of these arguments were summarised by the mediaeval philosopher and theologian, Thomas Aquinas. But all of them are open to objections as strict proofs. They are by nature pointers rather than proofs, and seem to support the convictions of believers, rather than pushing unbelievers into a logical corner from which there is no escape.

But the picture the world presents is ambiguous, with its mixture of beauty and ugliness, pleasure and pain. For an accidental world might not appear so very different, outwardly, from a planned world that has been spoiled by sin. One philosopher, John Hick, illustrates this ambiguity in a parable, 'The Road'. He writes of two men who are travelling along a road. One believes it leads to a Celestial City and the other does not. The first interprets the delights of the journey as encouragements sent by the king. The difficulties he takes as trials of his faith to make him a better citizen of the City. The second sees the journey as purposeless, but enjoys the good and endures the bad. Their expectations of the journey are the same but they differ about its destination. In the end, as they turn the last corner, it is apparent that one was right and the other was wrong.

The parable illustrates not only the apparent ambiguity of life's journey, but also the key issue of whether or not a belief is true. The travellers' two sets of belief about the world cannot both be true: they are mutually incompatible. In an age when relativism is very fashionable, this needs to be kept in mind.

The mixture of good and evil encountered on life's travels is claimed by some to deny the existence of a God of love. Others say the world was made perfect by a loving God, but went badly wrong because people disobeyed him. But those who make this last claim are going beyond what may be read off from the world we live in. They are claiming that God has revealed this to us – which brings us to another source of evidence met with in connection with religious belief, Revealed Theology.

Revealed Theology
This is based on the claim that God has told us things we could not have known by our reason or senses alone.

Such communication goes beyond reason and observation, rather than being necessarily contrary to them. The difference between Natural Theology and Revealed Theology may be compared to that between what we can find out about a person by direct investigation and what that person needs to tell us if we are to know it at all.

Christians claim that God has spoken through human mouthpieces, their messages being recorded in the Bible. But how can one know whether such claims are true? One might be persuaded by reading the Bible and experiencing what the translator J B Phillips called the 'ring of truth'. Such a sense of personal conviction is not insignificant, but our concern here is whether there are tests of a more public nature, tests that may be applied to what some claim God has revealed.

There *are* some tests, and they apply in other areas besides religious belief. One can ask whether the belief system is *consistent* – that is, is it free from internal contradictions? Then, if our limited experience ties up with what we learn when in a position to make a test, we gain confidence about aspects that we have not been able to test.

This was so with Michael Faraday's early experiences in chemistry. As a young person Faraday was much influenced by a book written by a Mrs Marcet called *Conversations in Chemistry*. He wrote:

> when I questioned Mrs. Marcet's book by such little experiments as I could find means to perform and found it true to the facts as I could understand them, I felt I had got hold of an anchor in chemical knowledge and clung fast to it. (Quoted in A Boorse & L Motz (eds) *The World of the Atom*, vol I, 1966, p 316, Basic Books)

Faraday was more ready to believe, on the authority of Mrs Marcet, those things he had not yet tested, because where he *had* been able to make tests, the results fitted in with what he had been told. So too, in religious matters, positive checks can increase our confidence in other, untested parts.

Another test is to see whether a system of beliefs holds together and makes sense overall, that is, whether it is *coherent*. When the beliefs come from a book like the Bible, written by some forty different authors over a period of about fifteen hundred years, is there nevertheless a unity, a coherence, about the message?

Thirdly, one can ask whether the system of beliefs covers the whole range of human experience – whether it is *comprehensive*. In the case of religious beliefs, does it deal with dying as well as living, with pain as well as pleasure?

Interpreting evidence

First-century Christian evidence consisted of eyewitness accounts. Since then, extensive documentation left by believers has given us their testimonies. But, inevitably, evidence must be interpreted. An illustration of this is provided by the early credal statement, 'Christ died for our sins' (1 Corinthians 15:3). The phrase 'Christ died' is supported from both secular and biblical sources; it is something beyond reasonable historical doubt. 'Christ died for our sins', however, is a Christian interpretation of the fact of his death, telling us what its purpose was. It certainly depends on the historical event of his death but, going beyond that, it draws, for its justification, upon evidence derived from the consistency, coherence and comprehensiveness of the total picture of Christ's life.

Although interpretation is inevitable, it would be wrong to think that the magic word 'interpretation' can be used to blow a smoke-screen across all attempts to find truth. One interpretation is *not* just as good as another. The historical data will allow some interpretations and not others; there is a need to search for the 'best fit'. This is certainly true of the historical data associated with the resurrection. It is especially important that evidence for this key event should be scrutinised carefully, since so much depends upon it. Professor Bruce concluded his book *The New Testament Documents* with these lines:

> The earliest propagators of Christianity welcomed the fullest examination of the credentials of their message. The events which they proclaimed were, as Paul said to King Agrippa, not done in a corner, and were well able to bear all the light that could be thrown on them. The spirit of these early Christians ought to animate their modern descendants. (F F Bruce *The New Testament Documents*, 1970, pp 119f, IVP)

Evidence – sufficient for action

Although there are no knock-down proofs, Christians for the last two millenia have judged that there is sufficient evidence for action. They have concluded with Paul that 'Christ has indeed been raised from the dead' and they have entered into a relationship, with the risen Christ, called 'eternal life'.

It is a cardinal mistake to think that Christ's physical resurrection may be discarded, and yet that the remaining doctrines can still do 'business as usual'. The resurrection is not an optional extra to Christianity, to be taken on board if found attractive and discarded if deemed unpalatable. It is the pivotal miracle of the faith. Christ's resurrection is the guarantee, for Christians, that his sacrifice for our sins was accepted, that death has lost its sting and the grave has been robbed of its victory, and that they, too, will be raised to everlasting life. So it is not surprising that, each Easter day, Christians the world over joyfully repeat the ancient response, 'He is risen indeed!'

Summary

We have looked at the biblical teaching about God's activity in the world and noted that this activity extends to normal events just as much as miraculous ones. Hence his working is not to be seen as confined to the gaps in current scientific explanations. The nature of science and its laws – which describe the normal courses of events – do not tell us whether or not miracles can happen. No satisfactory argument against miracles can be mounted by appealing to the working assumption of scientists – the Uniformity of Nature. The weaknesses of an argument of this kind – and of other arguments against miracles – have been rehearsed. In short, our current understanding of science provides no justification for denying the miraculous. Science contains many mysteries, a fact that should encourage humility rather than unwarranted dogmatism over contentious matters such as miracles.

The issue of whether or not miracles have happened is primarily an historical, rather than a scientific one. Appeals are made to a variety of forms of evidence, indirect and cumulative.

In conclusion, there appear to me to be no firm grounds for disbelieving the biblical miracle accounts. Nor are there grounds, in Scripture, for denying their role alongside the preaching of the gospel, as a means of convincing people that the power of God is still at work today.

12

When miracles don't happen

Sandy: I clearly remember how glad I felt when Bill made that remarkable recovery, after they prayed for him that Sunday evening at church. But that was before Trudy got cancer – they prayed for her too! It seems like yesterday, but it's over two years since she died, and I'm beginning to doubt whether I'll ever get over it.

Alistair: I can't say much. I'm as baffled as you are. I don't know why some people are healed and others aren't. Is it a lack of faith, or what?

Sheila: I don't want to sound unsympathetic, Sandy, but I look at it rather differently. I can't deny your friend Bill's recovery after that Sunday evening, but I think it's all psychological – mind over matter, or something of the sort. *I* can't believe it's God because, if he's all-powerful and all-good, everyone would be healed.

Within one domain of our lives – the *cognitive* one, which involves our reasoning, knowing and understanding – the issue of miracles may be subjected to critical analysis. We can grapple with nomenclature and definitions. We can analyse the concept of 'miracle' and classify miracles into types. We can examine and attempt to rebut the philosophical and scientific objections to the concept. We can research reports of miracles and we can quantify the extent of this type of spiritual experience. We can examine the extent of the evidence for alleged miraculous occurrences, attempting to evaluate the grounds for claiming that they occur, according to accepted canons of historical enquiry.

But in another domain of our lives – the *affective* one, which involves our feelings, reactions and responses – the issue of miracles can be a poignant, personal problem. The believer in a miracle-working God is likely to experience its cutting edge most keenly in a situation where the timely occurrence of a miracle could avoid tragedy – but nothing happens. This arises most commonly in connection with the illness and death of loved ones.

The painful line of reasoning is a simple one, repeated with variations many times over, and it goes something like this: 'The Bible is full of passages which assure us that God loves us more than any earthly father. It says, "the Lord will keep you from all harm" (Psalm 121). Yet now this has happened and I am so grieved I can hardly speak. I wouldn't have brought this on *my* children, so how do I reconcile my experience with my beliefs?'

The time to try to think such things through – for there are no simple answers – is either before such a trauma comes upon us, or long after. What we need at the time is a loving arm around our shoulders and someone who will weep alongside us, listen to our blurtings out, and neither repeat what we have said nor say too much themselves.

. . . language, as anyone who has ever tried to write to the newly bereaved must know, is insufficient even when handled with the skill of a poet and the sympathy of a friend: only immediate and living contact, the touch of life upon life can transmit a true report. (C E Raven *Science, Religion, and the Future*, 1968, p 13, CUP)

In the Old Testament account of Job's trials, his comforters did well at first – 'they began to weep aloud . . . they sat on the ground with him for seven days and seven nights. No-one said a word to him, because they saw how great his suffering was' (Job 2:12f). It was only when they opened their mouths, in platitudes and in error, that God rebuked them.

Theory and practice

The difference between the theory and reality of suffering is crystal clear in C S Lewis's two books, *The Problem of Pain* and *A Grief Observed*. The first, written prior to personal tragedy, was a valuable attempt to grapple with the mystery of suffering and it contains much helpful analysis. The second was the outpourings of Lewis's heart at the death of his recent bride, Joy Davidman. In a quite different way, it too is helpful, illustrating how inadequate the analysis of concepts is when one is in the depths of despair. Among many poignant passages, Lewis's comments on 'getting over it' are especially memorable:

Getting over it so soon? But the words are ambiguous. To say the patient is getting over it after an operation for appendicitis is one thing; after he's had his leg off it is quite another. After that operation either the wounded stump heals or the man dies . . . At present I am learning to get about on crutches. Perhaps I shall presently be given a wooden leg. But I shall never be a biped again. (p 43)

Similar thoughts were expressed by Stephen Verney, Canon of Windsor, in a radio broadcast. Through this talk came an affirmation of confidence, because of hope in what is a key miracle – the resurrection of Jesus Christ:

> Three years ago, my wife died of cancer. I am speaking
> now most directly to those who have passed through
> a similar experience, and, first of all, to say: 'You don't
> get through it quickly'. People say, 'He's marvellous',
> or, 'She's come to terms with it.' But, of course, you
> haven't. Some part of yourself has been torn out, and
> you fall to pieces, and gradually – very gradually –
> you have to be re-formed in a new pattern.
>
> But, from these first three years, I can truly say that
> this process of mourning is not just pain. It is also
> the discovery of new strength and new happiness, so
> that it can be not only the most terrible anguish, but,
> at the same time, the greatest privilege. The heart of
> this privilege has been the gradual unfolding of the
> mystery of resurrection . . . the story of the resurrection
> of Christ helped me to understand my wife's death,
> but, at the same time . . . her death has helped me to
> understand the resurrection of Christ. (Stephen
> Verney 'The mystery of resurrection', *The Listener*, 3
> March 1977, pp 273f)

But this book is not primarily concerned with the problems
of pain and suffering. Vast subjects like these need a book
to themselves. Nevertheless, suffering is inextricably linked
with the subject of miracles – or rather of their lack – as
Sheila's last remark shows. Her comment contains the glib
accusation that God cannot be all-powerful and also all-
good. If he is all-powerful and can heal, yet does not, he
is not all-good. If he is all-good and wants to heal, but
cannot, he is not all-powerful. It trips easily off the tongue,
yet fails to take account of the degree to which God has
made people part of his purposes. Their obedience and
faith help to fulfil his plans; their rebellion and unbelief
hinder them.

I am conscious that if major suffering comes into my
life before I have finished these last two chapters, analysis

and argument will, for the time being, seem irrelevant to me. But the task of thinking through what we believe must be attempted as part-fulfillment of 'the first and greatest commandment' which includes loving God 'with all your mind' (Matthew 22:37–38). So first we will take a rather detached and slightly caricatured look at ways in which some people react to the absence of miracles.

Why no miracles?

At one end of the spectrum of responses there are those who expect nothing and receive nothing. Of them it has been said, rather insensitively, 'Blessed are those that expect nothing: for they shall never be disappointed' – the text will not be found in Matthew 5! The theology of such people has no place for miracles today – or any other time, perhaps.

Then there are their opposites, who seem to expect a miracle-a-minute. They will lay hands on almost anyone, anywhere, and declare them to be healed. Some neighbours of ours experienced this superficial treatment when seeking help over the husband's leukaemia: the husband was pronounced healed but died shortly afterwards.

Such apparent anomalies may be accounted for in a variety of ways – all of which can claim some biblical justification. 'If you are sick and are not healed, it is because of your own lack of faith, or else some unconfessed sin.' This causes much additional anguish to those who are already in distress through illness. Desperate attempts to whip up more faith, or to trawl their subconscious for forgotten sins, only increase their misery. Although it is true that, in some villages mentioned in the New Testament, Jesus 'did not do many miracles there because of their lack of faith' (Matthew 13:58), there are other instances in which the faith, or lack of faith, of the individual is not even mentioned (Matthew 12:9–14), and there are also instances in which healing is given before the matter of sin is dealt with (John 5:1–14).

It is very easy, with such a bank of potential 'blocks' to miraculous healing, to insulate one's theology of 'healing always' against any possibility of being shown to be incorrect. For in any individual case, no one can be absolutely sure whether one or more of these 'blocks' is present and, if it is, whether that is responsible for the lack of healing.

It is also easy to insulate one's theology against falsification by shifting one's definition of 'miracle', or 'healing', in the middle of a discussion. Let me give an example of such a 'mid-course' redefinition for each of these words, starting with 'miracle'.

A children's talk at our church started with the story of the healing of the crippled beggar in Acts 3. Another story was then told, of a crippled child, in an overseas church, who needed an artificial leg. Against great financial odds, a group of poor people raised the large sum of money needed. This was referred to by the preacher as a 'miracle' and was presumably thought to illustrate the story in Acts.

In fact the telling of the second story contained a shift in the way the word 'miracle' was being used. The common factor in the two stories was that something wonderful had happened. In Acts it was a physical healing by the power of God which resulted in a lame man being restored to full health, able to walk and jump. In the second case, no miraculous healing was involved. What was wonderful in that case was the devotion of the poor people; it was so great that they were able to raise a large sum of money to enable a crippled person to move about artificially.

With the word 'healing', one example of shifting its meaning is the artifice I have heard used on a number of occasions. For instance, a sick woman is prayed for and yet she dies. Someone points out the obvious and painful fact that she was not healed. Someone else contradicts, saying that 'she was healed *really*, because God has taken her to be with himself, where there is no more pain'. The word 'healing' is here being used in two different senses.

When the first meaning, the restoration of the body to physical or mental health, is not realised, the meaning is changed, in order to save the theology. In philosophy this is called a *definitional retreat*.

I believe both these extreme positions – 'healing never' and 'healing always' – to be at variance with Scripture. When the kingdom of heaven draws near, when the Holy Spirit makes Christ known through the preaching of the good news, miracles – and not only healing ones – are to be expected and should be sought. Furthermore, I am convinced we should be seeing more of them than we do. Perhaps one reason for the dearth of miracles is the rather sickly state of the church in many places. Its public image does not gleam with life and confidence. One has a sneaking suspicion that the unbeliever distinguishes the genuine from the spurious more clearly than some who make public pronouncements in the name of the Church of Christ. Where this happens the church becomes an object of derision, unlikely to be persecuted, merely despised.

There was an illustration of this in the entertaining television series *Yes, Prime Minister* in the 1980s. One of its satires was devoted to the appointment of bishops, and a particular nominee was being favoured because to appoint him would 'restore the balance'. In reply to the question, 'What balance?' the answer was given, 'Between those who believe in God and those who don't.' The fact that this could have raised such a laugh from the audience said a great deal about the public perception of the church.

The life of the church has been changing significantly over the last few decades, although there is still a large disparity between contemporary church life (in many places) and that of the early church. This upsurge of life has attracted limited media publicity, but because controversy and peculiarity are the bread and butter of popular appeal and high viewing ratings, much ecclesiastical reporting focuses on the odd and the bizarre.

The reappearance of enthusiasm in the life of many

churches is splendid. If we are not ourselves enthusiastic, how are others likely to be attracted? 'Christianity is caught, not taught.' But enthusiasm without power can be a real 'turn-off'. After some so-called 'healing meetings', I have been left with the impression of having sat through a performance, in which little of lasting consequence has taken place. Many good Christians seem to me to be gullible in their response to some of these meetings. It is clearly healthier, and more honest, when miracles do not take place, to ask why they don't, rather than to engage in a superficial pretence that they *have* occurred.

Finding a balance

Knowing that miracles do take place, I want to discover how the church can move further into realising God's power in its midst today. There are no slick answers – it has to be worked out through prayer (and where necessary, fasting) in individual instances. But personal predispositions complicate the issue for many people: those brought up in particular (dispensational) church traditions may find it difficult to accept the possibility of spiritual gifts today, while those from traditions that concentrate strongly on signs and wonders may lose sight of God's action in everyday things.

I am often aware that people's understanding of the Bible can be bound up, as if by a powerful straitjacket, by their own personal predispositions and by tradition. In many cases, where a tradition appears to be at variance with the Scriptures, *that* tradition seems to override the Bible, even among Christians who claim the Bible as their sole guide to faith and practice.

Part of the reason for this seems to be that nowadays some Christians have only the most superficial grasp of the Bible. For some this results in tradition overriding the Bible, with the subsequent danger that they fail to enter fully into God's promises. For others, experience, rather than the Bible, takes precedence, which makes them vulnerable to experiences that do not come from the Spirit of God. In both cases people may be unaware of a subtle reversal of priorities. The first group emphasises 'basics', but is low on expectation of God's power at work among them. The second group emphasises experience at the expense of basic teaching. In both cases, Bible knowledge is selective.

Beginning in the 1950s, the charismatic revival moved many Christians away from a purely intellectual understanding of the faith, to something which is experiential and which meshes in with real life – a vital and long-overdue emphasis. Frequently, however, the recovery of a particular emphasis leads to a pendulum effect in which something that is also important becomes undervalued. Whereas it was the experience of the gifts and the power of the Holy Spirit that was under-emphasised, now it seems that repentance and salvation through the Cross of Christ are underplayed, together with the need to be thoroughly grounded in the Scriptures. I have puzzled, after attending meetings in which the Bible and prayer hardly seemed to feature at all, as to what was the 'cement' that bonded the group together. The words 'Bind us together with cords that cannot be broken' are often sung, but in practice how much of such binding is divinely provided, and how much is just the natural enjoyment of friends being together? Church history amply illustrates how Christian groups which emphasise experience to the neglect of biblical underpinning fall easy prey to heresy, imbalance and false prophecy, and are precarious in times of persecution. Experience is vital, but so is biblical understanding – a powerful church lives in the strength of them both. And it is only a powerful church that functions as the Body of Christ is intended to do – as a source of comfort and strength and as a people among whom spiritual gifts, such as those of healing, are exercised.

The 'Body of Christ'

The command to rejoice with those who rejoice and weep with those who weep (Romans 12:15) finds its intended fulfilment in a corporate context. The metaphor of the church as the Body of Christ focuses attention on the closeness with which individual Christians are intended to function together. Many Christians treat the church more as a club than as a body, to be attended – if you feel like it – on Sundays and then only if there is something interesting provided at the 'service'. The picture of the church as a body is very different: here the members hold to one another as each one holds to Christ as the head.

Suffering in one part of the physical body causes pain throughout the body, and help comes from other parts. If you hit your thumb with a hammer, the whole body feels out of gear. The same thing applies to pleasure. If you sit with your feet in hot water after a hike on a cold day, the whole body feels the glow. In a similar way members of a church 'body' will, ideally, respond speedily to each other. It is essential to live according to this intimate picture of organic church life, if the body is to be ready to rejoice and to comfort when necessary. We are easily caught on the hop, aware only of corporate unprepared-ness.

Sometimes we may ask, 'Why don't we see miracles in *our* church?' and fail to discern the spiritual poverty behind our smooth-running 'services'. Regular repentance towards God, confessing our faults to one another, tasting afresh the power of the Cross to reconcile and renew, are all prerequisites to being filled with the 'Holy Spirit, who is given to those who obey him'. This is the Christian norm rather than an impossible ideal, and where obedience is wholehearted, love will be genuine. From my limited experience, it appears to be in the churches where there is this genuine and costly love (rather than just friendly enquiries after your health on Sundays) that miracles happen, as a by-product of the overflowing life of God in his people.

At any moment, however, we may find ourselves in a situation in which a miracle is desperately sought. If it doesn't come, the responses of the *head* will be overtaken by the responses of the *heart*, and all kinds of pastoral problems follow. We will think about these problems in the last chapter.

13

Too shattered to think straight!

Husband: I've tried to understand why this should have happened to us, but it baffles me. It's the first time in my life I've felt abandoned by God. I don't *really* think I have been, but it seems like it at times. I've got to learn to trust more.

Wife: Yes, I keep going over the events again and again, asking myself whether there's anything more we could have done, any way we went wrong, but I get nowhere. My mind is like a tape recorder. I know every tiny detail vividly. I go over and over the same ground again, in the same sequence, until I come up against the same impenetrable brick wall and my head actually seems to hurt physically.

Whether suffering arises through disappointment that a miracle did not materialise, or through other troubles, the pastoral problems are similar. Part of 'the problem of pain' is that, with a variety of possible interpretations of tragedy, the facts on which we have to adjudicate are ambivalent. The premature death of a loved one may be seen as neglect by a supposedly loving heavenly Father; it may also be seen as an onslaught of the Enemy against an effective Christian who threatened the kingdom of darkness.

Make or break?

Intense suffering, whatever form it takes, is a watershed. It can make or break people, depending on one crucial matter. Just as, with a stream, one small geographical feature causes the water to rush down one side of a mountain rather than the other, so our perception of what lies behind the tragedy may make a crucial difference. To change the metaphor, it may tip the balance, so we either rise to the heights or descend to the depths.

One Christian couple I know of lost one of their two sons in a motor-cycle accident. Formerly active in their church, they moved away and withdrew more and more from any Christian activity. But another Christian couple I know, who lost their only son in a car accident, are still going on strongly with God.

The expectations of Christians in much of the Western world are very different from those of Christians in totalitarian countries. Material blessings, a good job, a spouse, two kids and a semi-detached in suburbia are commonly regarded as the new birthright. In the Bible, of course, there are plenty of verses containing God's promises to bless his people. But 'health and wealth' must seem strange expectations to an undernourished, physically abused prisoner-for-Christ, in a filthy cell far removed from the affluent West. Perhaps the promise that strengthens him or her, and gives vital reassurance, is that 'every one who wants to live a godly life in Christ Jesus will be persecuted' (2 Timothy 3:12).

The example of Job

The book of Job gives many helpful insights into suffering, opening our eyes to the spiritual warfare that lies behind human tragedy, and providing an example of how a godly man reacts to disaster. For instance, it is recorded of Job's initial response to his devastation that 'In all this, Job did not sin in what he said' (2:10). He exercised faith, and will, over immediate emotional response – 'Though he slay me, yet will I hope in him' (13:15). As the book proceeds, however, we also see that protracted suffering can cause even the faithful to despair.

Job's suffering was not on account of the faithlessness of God but on account of the faithfulness of Job. 'Job only butters you up, God, for what he gets out of it,' was the substance of Satan's taunt. God chose to prove him wrong, at great cost to Job but at great gain to God's purposes in showing the principles of his kingdom to the 'rulers and authorities in the heavenly realms' (Ephesians 3:10). Perhaps one of the most helpful features of the book is Job's total ignorance, throughout, of the ultimate cause of his suffering. There is no indication that he was ever told why he had been used as a punch-bag. So Job, like Abraham, had to walk by faith, not by sight – as Christians today must do.

Temptations at a time of crisis

For the Christian, trusting God at a time of great bewilderment is a tough challenge. But to duck such a challenge, to marginalise God on account of personal tragedy and then to find out, in the age to come, that it was not divine neglect but Satanic sifting that was the source of the sufferings, will cause the deepest regret. The person who fails in this way may well regret the wasted years, when their service for God has been suspicious and half-hearted, because they secretly doubted his total commitment to their good.

The initial wild, resentful resolve to 'chuck it all up' may not last long – especially if it isn't blurted out to all and sundry, so making retraction harder. But there is another temptation at this time, which is to 'keep up a front' in order to disguise inner alienation. In one way, some restraint on expressing our inner feelings is no bad thing, so that we do not make others stumble – hence my earlier comment about the need to restrict our less-controlled outpourings of grief to the ears of a few discreet comforters. The psalmist, when at an all-time spiritual low, kept his mouth shut, for, he reasoned, 'If I had said, "I will speak thus", I would have betrayed this generation of your children' (Psalm 73:15). In other ways, however, a 'front' is unhealthy, resulting in playacting (which is the meaning of hypocrisy). Officially we are trusting God, but if we are walking by sight and not by faith we may well be aware of how deeply *mis*trustful we are, keeping God at arm's length. Instead of knowing his love to be enfolding us, we feel rather – to lift Shakespeare's phrase – that we 'dwell in the suburbs of his good pleasure'.

What might God think about such a way of living? In view of his warning to the church at Laodicea, 'because you are lukewarm – neither hot nor cold – I am about to spit you out of my mouth', I suspect that the long-term tactic of holding God at arm's length is even more distasteful to him than short-lived shouts of angry complaint. I knew a Christian girl whose immediate response to being stood up by her boy-friend was to tear up her Bible – but it was not long before she asked for forgiveness.

Another reaction to grief is long-term wallowing in sorrow, a serious danger against which we are warned, '... see to it ... that no bitter root grows up to cause trouble and defile many' (Hebrews 12:15). To fail in this respect is to be like the one-talent man who frittered his opportunities away in resentment – 'I knew that you are a hard man, harvesting where you have not sown and gathering where you have not scattered seed' (Matthew 25:24). Such people have an air of death about them: the desert has encroached, and their life has all but drained away. Everywhere they go they seem to drain life out of everyone else.

Although God will patiently comfort people, in order gently to bring about their restoration, he doesn't always say comfortable things to us in our times of sorrow. Jeremiah's complaint to God about the prosperity of the wicked and his own plight was answered, not with soothing words, but with tough ones: 'If you have raced with men on foot and they have worn you out, how can you compete with horses? If you stumble in safe country, how will you manage in the thickets by the Jordan?' (Jeremiah 12:5). Not, perhaps, the comforting words he would have liked; just a terse reminder that he was living in spiritual wartime.

Confronted with pain and difficulties, some Christians will give up the Christian life altogether, and rationalise their new position by giving a reason that has nothing to do with the cause of their hurt. One Christian young man I knew had a distressing relationship with a girl while he was at college, and abandoned his faith. Later, in conversation, he put the whole of his previous Christian experience down to emotion. No one should point a finger of accusation; he was hurting deeply, and many of us have known the agony he experienced.

A biology teacher, whose friend had died, gave up her Christianity and rationalised her departure from the faith, saying, 'I am a scientist'. It would have been appropriate but insensitive to refer her to several Professors of Biology who maintain a robust Christian faith that meshes in with their studies. Her problem was not an intellectual one; she was hurting inside, and science was her rationalisation of the position she had adopted for other reasons.

Some of these real-life stories, which I have selected to make particular points, are discouraging; but they can serve us as cautionary tales. Other stories of suffering have rich endings, and I want to conclude this book by telling about one person who bore much suffering, by the grace of God, in a way that encourages me every time I think about it.

A splendid man

My story is of a friend whom I often remember in connection with suffering and the positive effects of receiving it rightly. As a young man, he went abroad to be a missionary and married a Christian national. Not long afterwards his wife began to show signs of mental instability and he made the heartbreaking decision to return home; his plans and calling seemed to lie in ruins. For twenty years he nursed her in her failing health and at the same time acted as a minister to an independent church. He confided how, Sunday by Sunday, as he set off to preach and encourage others, he told the Lord he could not go on. But by the strength and grace of God he did.

There emerged a man who was 'gold tried by the fire'. It was a joy to be in his presence; he was the kind of person to whom one could turn in real sorrow, knowing he would not give superficial answers. Remembering him one might echo Paul's words to his friends at Philippi, 'I thank God every time I remember you' (Philippians 1:3).

After his first wife's death he had a very happy second marriage, which lasted some years. Then his second wife contracted cancer, was wrongly diagnosed, and died within a fortnight. In his pain I am sure he would have echoed the words of the Scottish minister, Andrew Bonar, at the death of his wife.

He does not forbid me to mourn. Nor will he forget to bless.

The next two paragraphs were inserted after the earlier ones were written for, just a few days after writing them, I had a telephone call to say that this friend had died. The quality of his life, refined by the way he had received suffering, remained until the end. His last hours were typical of his life, which can be summarised by the acronym he used in the children's talks for which he was famous – J O Y – Jesus first, Others second, Yourself last.

Retiring to bed with a pain, he wrote a note, explaining his condition and leaving a few telephone numbers – 'in case they are needed': they were.

It had always been his wish and prayer that he should go to bed one night and, from there, straight to heaven. Like Paul, he finished his course with joy. I am reminded of the words of D L Moody, when he said, 'Some fine morning you will read in the newspapers, "D L Moody is dead". Don't believe it. I shall be more alive that morning than ever before.'

Building materials

St Paul draws an analogy between the way we live our lives and the way we might construct a building. We build either with consumables, which Paul likens to wood, hay and straw, or with valuable, permanent materials (1 Corinthians 3:10–15). He teaches that it is possible to 'be saved, but only as one escaping through the flames', all one's works having failed the test of permanency – a solemn thought. I once heard the preacher Lance Lambert speak on the imagery of the precious building materials which will survive to eternity – gold, precious stones and pearls. His thoughts stayed with me and I reproduce their substance as best I can after nearly thirty years.

Gold

This precious metal is refined by fire, as was my missionary friend. The intense heat of life's trials need not destroy us, but it can purify – if we will let it. It can turn us into those much needed pillars of the church, able to uphold others because we have ourselves been upheld. This thought also comes from Paul, who refers to God as 'the Father of compassion and the God of all comfort, who comforts us in all our troubles, so that we can comfort those in any trouble with the comfort we ourselves have received from God' (2 Corinthians 1:3–4). We need not have been through the same experience as those we want to comfort, only to have known for ourselves the comfort of the God who also wants to comfort them.

Precious stones

These occur in nature when common, unattractive materials like black carbon are subjected to tremendous heat and pressure in unseen places. What emerges is something desirable and attractive, such as a diamond. A popular chorus invites Jesus to take us as we are and to make us like precious stones 'crystal clear and finely honed'. Certainly God will take us as we are; but he will not leave us as we are. The honing can be painful. The results can be brilliant.

Pearls

A pearl, as is well known, is produced when a grain of sand gets inside an oyster. Gradually the irritating grain of sand will be clothed with layer upon layer of beautiful material, until it is transformed into something attractive and desirable. It is possible for a similar process to take place in an individual life, a source of irritation being gradually transformed into something beautiful.

Some of the saintliest people are found to have experienced protracted trials. They have learned that it is still possible to serve God and be a faithful witness, even with an aching heart. That which turns one person into an embittered stream of frustrations and complaints, transforms another into a mighty, rushing river of life. As to what might happen in *our* lives, in similar circumstances – the choice is ours.

APPENDIX

Resurrection under review

Since Christianity stands or falls by the resurrection of Jesus Christ, it is inevitable that this historical event should be closely scrutinised. This is neither surprising nor particularly newsworthy. Media attention *is* attracted, however, when people who occupy positions as guardians of the faith appear to be questioning aspects of its importance.

'I don't think it means a physical resurrection. It means spiritual resurrection, a transforming resurrection, a real resurrection,' said David Jenkins, Bishop of Durham, on Easter day, 1989. It is the kind of claim that radio, television and the press will seize upon as grist to the mill.

Assertions such as this have an element of *déjà vu* about them. Matthew Arnold, in the nineteenth century, appeared to be claiming some such privileged insight into first-century history when he confidently declared:

> That gracious Child, that thorn-crown'd Man!
> He lived while we believed.
> . . . .
> Now he is dead. Far hence he lies
> In the lorn Syrian town,

And on his grave, with shining eyes,
The Syrian stars look down.

Obermann Once More

But one wonders how Arnold could have supported his assertion!

Twenty years ago, John Robinson, then Bishop of Woolwich, offered some intellectual comfort to modern man now 'come of age' and supposedly unable to believe in resurrection. It was possible for him to

> be *free* to say that the bones of Jesus lie around somewhere in Palestine. . . . even if the corpse was somewhere around, as the cocoon is somewhere around when the butterfly has flown, it was as nothing to his friends any longer. (J A T Robinson *But That I Can't Believe!* 1967, pp 13, 39, Fontana)

So was Bishop Robinson, too, claiming inside information to which others were not party? Since there is now no way of checking whether 'it was as nothing to his friends' – and this runs contrary to the New Testament accounts – one could only read on. Apparently, it was supposed to be because the disciples sometimes had

> a sudden, startling conviction of Jesus's presence, as tangible as flesh and blood.
> At other times it was a more gradual recognition of him behind other eyes and other lips. (Robinson, *ibid*, p 39)

But to claim that 'the truth of the Resurrection is *a present experience*' from impressions like these, might be more than 'a plain, blunt man' – even one come of age – could take. If the corpse *was* 'somewhere around', an outside observer would probably conclude that recent events had been too much for the disciples, who were suffering from serious, if pleasant, delusions. To say of someone who is dead that you recognise him 'behind other eyes and other lips', is to say no more than that the way somebody looks and talks is like the way the dead person used to look and talk when he was alive. To claim more than that is to trade on the ambiguity of a figure of speech.

Two decades later, and for several years running at that, we are being told repeatedly that it really does not matter whether you believe in the physical resurrection of Jesus or not. Once more the speaker is a bishop, which is why his words attract particular attention.

In an early phase of the controversy David Jenkins, Bishop of Durham, explained his views to the General Synod of the Church of England, saying, 'The Resurrection narratives are far more about encounters and namings and joyful recognitions than about the empty tomb.' (D E Jenkins *God, Miracle and the Church of England*, 1987, p 6, SCM Press) His claim is reminiscent of John Robinson's earlier one, that 'the conviction of Christ's living power – which is what belief in *the Resurrection* means – does not *turn* on any theory of what happened to the body.' To say that 'joyful recognitions' are more important than the empty tomb is one thing, but to downgrade the importance of the empty tomb is quite another. For if some distant grave *were* still occupied by Jesus, then there would have been no 'encounters' or 'joyful recognitions', only tragic illusions.

God, according to David Jenkins, would not have raised his Son physically because 'The choice of physical miracles with what might be called laser-beam-like precision and power would not seem to be a choice which He cared, or would care, to use.' (*ibid*, p 5) But here again, as with Matthew Arnold and John Robinson, David Jenkins seems to be claiming some privileged insight. How else could he know that God would not care to use physical miracles? A reading of the New Testament does nothing to support such a speculation. Dr Jenkins promptly offered an explanation: God would not have cared to use such methods, otherwise he would have been prepared to use them to stop major suffering in the world.

Certainly the problem of suffering is a vast subject; many people will be aware of the theological debates concerning divine love, divine omnipotence and human free-will. But whether or not the resurrection took place is an *historical* matter which is independent of theological difficulties of this kind, and also of the ability of 'man come of age' to believe it. The danger here is that of making *our* understanding of God, and *our* expectations about what he will do, the measure of what he *actually* does. To do so is to resort to rationalistic arguments.

To describe the resurrection as God performing a 'conjuring trick with bones', as David Jenkins has done, both trivialises and prejudges the resurrection. The metaphor is poorly chosen. Conjuring is done for entertainment; resurrection is 'deadly' serious. It might, after all, turn out that God is not so predictable and pocket-sized as we might like. A god-in-a-box is convenient, because he can be made to perform at the press of a button – to everyone else's surprise, but not to those 'in the know'. But the God whose thoughts are higher than our thoughts and whose ways are higher than our ways, is much more uncomfortable to live with. We might not have him 'taped' after all.

Is modern man so much wiser than his forebears? The ancients were not stupid. They knew very well that it was not normal for virgins to have sons or for dead people to rise. So has 'man come of age' grown arrogant, making his own understanding the measure of divine ability? Isn't his attitude like that of some growing child who, intoxicated with the first taste of knowledge, thinks he knows everything? The problem of the resurrection may not be that modern man knows too much, but that he understands too little.

'Newspeak'

One of the difficulties associated with theological pronouncements like the ones referred to, is the use of language. Certainly, ordinary language is inadequate in many ways for discussing God, and often it is necessary to use figures of speech. But one has the impression, even after careful scrutiny of what is being said, that words usually used by orthodox theologians are here being used in such a different way that different words should be used. 'Newspeak' is as potentially dangerous in theology as in the politics of Orwell's *1984* – more so, in fact, since the issues are of greater consequence.

In the case in question, it has been claimed that resurrection is not being denied. But confusion can easily arise if 'resurrection' is used as a 'portmanteau' word, into which almost anything can be packed at will. To most people, whether they believe it happens or not, resurrection means the coming to life of a dead, physical body. If it is claimed that someone has died, been placed in a tomb, and has then been resurrected, most people would have a particular expectation – that that person's corpse will not be found in the tomb or anywhere else. If it were found, the word 'resurrection' would not be used, since it means a restoration to physical life. Certainly the Bible indicates that the resurrection involved more than simply a restoration of the physical body of Jesus. There *was* a transformation, but the transformed Jesus had a bodily continuity with the corpse that had been laid in the tomb.

David Jenkins says, in defence of his position, 'it is no mere figure of speech . . . to speak of the people of God as the body of Christ; for this is the place where Jesus is embodied now, where he is to be encountered.' The splendid metaphor of the Church as the Body of Christ is here being misused. For the meaning of the term 'Body of Christ' is being shifted, right in the middle of a discussion about the resurrection of Christ's body, to its metaphorical application to the Body of Christ – the Church. The 'sleight of hand' must not go undetected. Perhaps it would be a little improper to call it 'a conjuring trick with words', but the comparison does suggest itself. There is a danger in using theological imagery, such as 'the Body of Christ', in such a way as to contradict other parts of scripture.

Murray Harris, in a helpful examination of David Jenkins' views, draws attention to the Bishop's 'failure to distinguish the reactions of the disciples from the prior experience of Jesus'. He sums up by saying:

> The basic flaw of such a view is that it confuses the nature and the effect of the resurrection. The disciples' emerging conviction that Jesus 'was in fact not dead and finished, but alive and purposefully active' . . . was not itself the resurrection of Jesus but the result of the resurrection. According to the New Testament the resurrection of Jesus was his bodily and permanent emergence from death in a transformed state, and his exaltation to God's right hand. When the empty tomb and appearances of Jesus had made it clear that he had been reanimated and transformed, faith in the risen Jesus was born in his followers. We must never lose sight of the necessary distinction between the resurrection fact and the resurrection faith. (M J Harris *Easter in Durham*, 1985, p 31, Paternoster)

It is misleading to deny a bodily resurrection and yet to speak of Christ's 'risenness' or of 'his livingness on the other side of his death'. Expressions like 'encounters', 'namings' and 'joyful recognitions' are inappropriate, except in a limited metaphorical sense, which must be understood separately from a bodily meeting with a person, or any process of pattern-recognition with physical eyes.

To conclude with a general point about biblical interpretation: using imagery does not make it possible to have one's theological cake and eat it. Sometimes contradictions are disguised with ponderous phrases like, 'there is a very real sense in which' or, 'but in much deeper way, it could be said'. This can result in a kind of theological 'one-upmanship', where the hearer is made to feel he must be shallow in his thinking. In fact he may just be a victim of what C S Lewis once called 'Fern-seeds and Elephants', an aberration in those who 'claim to see fern-seed and can't see an elephant ten yards away in broad daylight.' It is possible to use erudite language and yet to miss the obvious. This is in no way a criticism of theology. Theology is an important and scholarly activity, and I have theologian colleagues whose scholarship I value. It is simply a comment on the kind of religious thinking which could be construed as being on a par with a long and undistinguished tradition which will 'strain at a gnat, and swallow a camel' (Matthew 23:24).

Further reading

Anderson, J N D *The Evidence for the Resurrection* (reprint of 1st ed.), 1988, Leicester: Inter-Varsity Press
Brown, C *Miracles and the Critical Mind*, 1984, Exeter: Paternoster Press
Harris, M J *Easter in Durham*, 1985, Exeter: Paternoster Press
Walker, A (ed) *Different Gospels*, 1988, London: Hodder & Stoughton
Ward, K *Evidence for the Virgin Birth*, 1987, London: Mowbray